Feng Shui:

a Hong Kong Perspective

Feng Shui:
a Hong Kong Perspective

by Dr Jin Peh

Feng Shui Columnist
for the South China Morning Post

GOLDEN HOARD PRESS
2010

Published by Golden Hoard Press Pte Ltd
PO Box 1073
Robinson Road PO
Singapore 902123

www.goldenhoard.net/fengshui.htm

HK distribution:
11th floor
3 to 7A Prat Avenue
Tsim Sha Tsui
Hong Kong

First Edition

ISBN: 978-0-9557387-9-1

Printed in Malaysia

Contents

Introduction

Chapter 1: Feng Shui Theory

Chapter 2: The Bedroom

Chapter 3: Children and Pregnancy

Chapter 4: Colours, Numbers and Water

Chapter 5: Date Selection

Chapter 6: Festivals

Chapter 7: Decorations and Symbols

Chapter 8: Doors and Windows

Chapter 9: Exteriors

Chapter 10: Feng Shui Calculations

Chapter 11: Internal Shapes and Structures

Chapter 12: Mirrors

Chapter 13: The Office and Work

Chapter 14: Other Rooms

Chapter 15: Spiritual Matters

Chapter 16: Chinese Astrology

Chapter 17: Chinese Names

Introduction

Dr Jin Peh grew up in Singapore and moved to Perth, Western Australia, as a teenager. Here he completed his medical training and internship, graduating as a doctor in 1996. He then took an Associate Degree in Broadcasting Journalism at the West Australian Academy of Performing Arts, which counts Hugh Jackman among its alumni. He became interested in the Chinese art of feng shui while working as a radio announcer, news reader and journalist.

He ended up spending two years in Taipei, Taiwan, as part of his apprenticeship with the renowned feng shui master Charlie Chen, who specialises in both Yang and Yin House (residence and grave) feng shui. Following his apprenticeship, Jin then proceeded to learn the Flying Stars School of feng shui from another renowned feng shui master. The emphasis throughout Jin's feng shui training has been on Classical feng shui, schools like the Three Harmony, Three Periods, Nine Stars, 64 Hexagrams Da Gua and the Flying Stars Schools.

Jin is also well versed in the use of the traditional feng shui compass or *luo pan*, which is applied to both Yang and Yin Houses feng shui. Jin has been based in Dubai for the last seven years, and has carried out feng shui assessments in countries as diverse as Singapore, Malaysia, Indonesia, Hong Kong, Australia, USA, Canada, Switzerland, Germany, Kuwait, Bahrain and the United Arab Emirates.

Since March 2005, he has been the resident Feng Shui columnist and expert with the *South China Morning Post*, the major English newspaper in Hong Kong.

The author can be contacted at jinpeh@doramail.com.

Chapter 1

Feng Shui Theory

White Tiger, Green Dragon (Creature Features)

You have probably heard of the following animals when it comes to describing the environment surrounding your home: the tiger, the dragon, the tortoise and the phoenix.

These four 'celestial animals' are used to signify the front, back and sides of a residence, and they have practical applications in feng shui. It would be wrong, however, to assume a specific creature relates to a specific direction.

The 'black tortoise' refers to mountains behind a property. Thus, when looking out from the front door, it's best to have supportive black tortoises, or buildings taller than yours, at the back. The 'red phoenix' refers to the area that lies in front of a building; it should be lower to provide support.

The 'green dragon' side lies to your left when you are facing the front door of a home when inside; the 'white tiger' lies to your right. The dragon side reflects the male influence in a property and the tiger side the female.

In apartments where the dragon side is more prominent (that is, taller or longer), men tend to be in charge, and more sons are conceived. Conversely, properties with the tiger side more pronounced see women as the stronger presence and have a higher ratio of daughters.

There are techniques to redress any such unwanted imbalances, but they are complicated.

Column No 27: September 4, 2005

Different Schools of Feng Shui 1 (School's Out)

Many people with a passing interest in feng shui have come across terms such as 'Flying Stars' and 'Eight Mansions' without fully understanding what they mean. Feng Shui has many classical schools, each with its own fervent group of supporters.

There has recently been a proliferation of non-classical feng shui theories, which are prevalent in western books on the subject but are not found in classical feng shui texts. The validity and effectiveness of such schools has been inconsistent and, questionable.

For example, one school suggests the southwest corner of a house - regardless of orientation and age - is always associated with romance.

Classically trained feng shui consultants will not just use such simple fixed rules of thumb, but will take into account the environmental (visible) and astrological and chronological (invisible) influences of an area when carrying out an audit.

For instance, they will place the bed not only in a sector that is appropriate for the client, but also out of the path leading from the door or toilet. They will avoid placing the bed below a window or with the door behind it. Practitioners who focus only on one type of influence without taking the others into account render themselves vulnerable to poor results.

Column No 56: April 9, 2006

Different Schools of Feng Shui 2 (Written in the Stars)

The branch of feng shui that is most popular in Hong Kong is the Flying Stars School, known in Cantonese as the *Fei Hsing Fa*. It takes into account the position of a property, when it was built, and also the years of birth of the individuals living or working therein. There are nine stars, which fly in a specific sequence, each representing a different quality, such as romance, academic achievement, wealth, illness or mishap.

Another traditional branch of feng shui is the San He (Three Combinations or Harmony) school, which takes into account an individual's astrological birth data. Depending on the master, either the year, the Four Pillars or the Eight Characters of birth are used to determine a person's most favourable colours, directions and elements.

Finally, the Eight Mansions or *Ba Chai* method has also had a lot of coverage in English-language feng shui books. This school divides individuals into two groups (east and west) depending on calculations based on the year of birth. Four auspicious and four inauspicious directions are then assigned to a person.

While there are strong advocates for this school, you should be aware of its practical limitations, one of which concerns the positioning of a bed when its occupants have opposing auspicious directions.

Column No 57: April 16, 2006

Feng Shui Ethics (False Idols)

Clients are advised to exercise caution when following the advice of feng shui consultants, especially if the advice results in significant disruption to their life. Like all professionals, feng shui masters should take responsibility for their suggestions and act ethically.

Professionals should be open about who they learned their trade from and the amount of time it took them to qualify. The term *jiang hu pai* (rivers and lakes sect) is used to describe charlatans who garnered their knowledge from books without serving an apprenticeship under an accomplished master.

Scrupulous masters will not suggest a client buy feng shui items from them, as this is clearly a conflict of interest. Classical feng shui masters did not try to sell statues, crystals or trinkets, especially those that have been 'personally energized' or 'blessed'. If feng shui items are required, they can be obtained from an independent shop in which the master has no financial interest.

Feng Shui masters should not suggest disruptive interventions, such as knocking down walls, or sleeping in a child's bunk bed, without taking into account the clients' opinions.

Feng Shui should improve the overall quality of your life and not create additional stress.

Column No 117: June 24, 2007

Units of Time (Time After Time)

In Chinese philosophy, time is cyclical. For instance, the signs of the Chinese zodiac repeat themselves every 12 years. From a feng shui perspective, there are different influences and in different hours, days, months and years.

The Flying Stars School is a traditional branch of feng shui that takes time into account. Essentially, time is divided into nine units - or periods - of 20 years each, giving a total of 180 years. It is believed energy completes a full cycle every 180 years, which is known in Putonghua as a *da yun*, or in Cantonese as a *dai wan*, a 'large period'. The term *yun* in this context has been translated into English as 'luck cycle', 'fortune' or 'age', creating much confusion for the casual reader. This system of measuring time has been used for almost 5,000 years; we are now in period eight of the 27th large period.

Periods are used in Flying Stars calculations to assess the energy of a property. Period seven ran from February 4, 1984, to February 4, 2004. Period eight started on February 4, 2004, and will run until February 4, 2024. Thus, two properties with the same orientation, for example, with one completed in 1996 (period seven) and the other in 2006 (period eight) will exert quite different effects on their occupants.

Column No 118: July 1, 2007

Facing South (Southern Exposure)

South facing properties are considered ideal, but Hong Kong residents don't know why. This concept is related more to the traditional method of building homes in ancient China than to feng shui principles.

In northern China, builders had to secure heat during the cold winters and minimize exposure to the sun during the hot summers. In addition, natural light had to be maximised throughout the year. The weather patterns also account for the fact traditional homes generally lacked windows on the northern, eastern or western walls and were protected in the rear by hills, if there were any, from the winter and spring winds.

In southern China and Hong Kong, where the summer is longer and the winter milder, windows face south or southeast to receive the wind from these directions during hot weather.

In modern times, thanks to air conditioning and central heating, it is not necessary to have your windows facing south. Adjacent buildings may also occupy the southward aspect of your apartment, thereby blocking sunlight and wind.

What is more important is that your balcony or other main windows face east to obtain the positive energy of the rising sun.

Column No 141: December 10, 2007

Different Spellings (In Other Words)

In some English articles and books about the subject, *feng shui* is spelled *fung shui*. Both *fung* and *feng* refer to the same Chinese character, one that means 'wind'. However, *fung* is the Cantonese pronunciation, while *feng* is the Putonghua pronunciation. As Cantonese is spoken predominantly in Hong Kong, the term *fung shui* is more widely understood there than *feng shui*. In Taiwan and parts of Southeast Asia, *feng shui* is known by its Hokkien pronunciation *hong sui*.

Energy, or *qi*, can also be spelled *chi*. Indeed, the terms *qigong* and *chi gong* are both commonly used. This can be attributed to the two main systems of romanisation that are used for Chinese characters. *Chi* is spelled using the Wade-Giles romanisation system, developed by Thomas Francis Wade, former British ambassador in Beijing and first professor of Chinese at Cambridge University, in the 1860s.

It was refined in 1912 by British diplomat Herbert Allen Giles. This system was used for many years by European scholars of Chinese culture, resulting in terms such as *tai chi* entering the popular lexicon. In contrast, *qi* is spelled in the Hanyu Pinyin system, which was officially adopted by the People's Republic of China in 1979 and is now widely taught to foreigners who are learning Putonghua.

Column No 144: January 6, 2008

Earth Luck (Feeling Lucky)

The Chinese believe there are three components to one's fortunes: Heaven luck, Earth luck and Man luck.

Heaven luck refers to the components of fate and fluctuations in fortune, essentially what a person is born with. Professional astrologers are able to deduce this from their time of birth. For instance, if you are fated to be a successful academic, you should not channel your efforts into becoming a politician or an entertainer. Even if you are in the right career, there will always be fluctuations in life. These are known as luck cycles and can also be identified from your birth chart.

Man luck is the manifestations of a person's principles. Thus, someone who lives his life with honesty and integrity will attract positive events while those whose ethics are flexible may experience setbacks. The amount of effort put into life will also affect a person's fortune: simply waiting for others to contact you with job offers without being proactive will not yield consistent results.

Finally, Earth luck refers to the effects of a person's working and living environment on their career and life. While feng shui is able to optimize this aspect of fortune, it is still no excuse to be complacent (ignoring Man luck) or have unrealistic expectations (relying on Heaven luck), as it is only one third of the overall picture.

Column No 154: March 23, 2008

Hemispheres (The North-South Divide)

There has been much debate in feng shui circles about different rules applying to those living in the northern and southern hemispheres. The proponents of the southern-hemisphere branch of feng shui argue that since the seasons and direction from which the sun is shining differ in their half of the planet, different rules should apply.

Houses face south in the northern hemisphere to obtain warmth from the sun while those in the southern hemisphere face north. Equipped with these observations, radical feng shui theories are then proposed, including the reversing of east and west in calculations and reversing the flight of the annual Flying Stars.

Traditional feng shui masters say the Sun still rises in the east, and north remains north regardless of which half of the planet one is in, and there is no reason to reverse calculations because a property is in the southern hemisphere.

It should also be noted that countries that straddle the equator, such as Indonesia and Kenya, do not exhibit two sets of characteristics – one for each side

Thus, those with family or friends living in Australia or South America should reassure them that traditional feng shui principles and calculations still apply to them.

Column No 159: April 27, 2008

The Water Dragon (Flow Charts)

You may have come across the term 'Water Dragon' when reading books about feng shui. These calculations determine the effects exerted by any water that is present around your living environment (streams and rivers, for example). Water flowing towards your home from a certain direction and exiting in another may bring forth good fortune and wealth, but if it flows in and exits from inappropriate sectors, then occupants may encounter health and financial problems.

In classical feng shui, the presence of water symbolized wealth. Hence, feng shui masters ensured the water present in a living environment was clean and fresh and approached a house from a beneficial sector. After establishing the orientation of the home through the use of the feng shui compass or *luo pan*, the next step would have been to use Water Dragon formulas to establish ideal positions for water to enter and exit.

For modern living, roads have replaced water in feng shui considerations, which is why the amount of traffic, as well as the direction of roads around your home, should be noted.

Some feng shui masters state that Water Dragon methods can be simulated by installing drains, but the costs of such measures are prohibitive.

Column No 161: May 11, 2008

Living Feng Shui (Flexible Approach)

While directions play a vital role in feng shui, they should not be followed to the extent that other factors are ignored. For instance, in Hindu culture, the dead are laid out with their heads pointing north, which explains why Hindus don't like to sleep in that direction.

While their beliefs and customs should be taken into account, it does not justify them sleeping with their heads pointing towards the door or in the path of the toilet, just to ensure their head face south. Feng Shui principles and personal beliefs must be considered as a whole.

Feng Shui is not an inflexible set of calculations and formulas that should be strictly adhered to at all times. It needs to take into account personal circumstances and preferences. For instance, if the most auspicious sector of a home is in the children's bedroom, the consultant should not insist the husband and wife sleep in there.

Feng Shui should never be applied in such a way as to create problems. The consultant should never forget that clients have to live with their advice. If you find yourself in a situation that is creating too much stress, maybe you should seek a second opinion.

Column No 184: October 19, 2008

The Bright Hall (For a Bright Future)

You may have come across the term *ming tang*, which means 'bright hall' or 'space', in a feng shui book. In classical texts, this refers to the open space in front of a home, which allows positive energy to accumulate, and then to enter when occupants use the main entrance.

This area should be sheltered from strong winds and should have sufficient lighting for the beneficial chi to remain. When the space lacks protection from the elements, the energy will be scattered, leaving the occupants feeling vulnerable and unsettled. If the open space has overgrown trees, excessive yin energy will be produced instead, resulting in occupants feeling lethargic and depressed.

Those living in apartments should have adequate space in front of the main entrance. Preferably, the main door should not open directly onto a solid wall, especially if the space between the door and the wall is so tight that moving furniture becomes difficult.

In these circumstances, occupants will encounter obstacles in their professional and personal lives. They will also lack foresight and exhibit short-term thinking.

The front door of your unit should also not be at the end of a long corridor, as this will leave occupants vulnerable to mishaps and accidents.

Column No 185: October 26, 2008

Empty Houses (Homecoming Blues)

Have you ever returned home from a long holiday to problems with the plumbing or electricity, or a suffocating feeling of flatness in the place?

Problems such as these can be attributed to an accumulation or of yin energy. Homes require human activity to increase the level of their yang energy.

If, for example, a mansion is inhabited by only one or two people, the occupants may feel lonely and be prone to pessimistic thoughts, lethargy and depression. Excessive yin will also lead to a higher incidence of conditions such as arthritis, night sweats and viral infections.

To raise the level of yang energy after a long period away from home, start by opening the curtains to introduce as much natural light as possible. Leaving the radio or television on will also help.

If your home is going to be empty for a few months, consider suggesting to family or close friends that they hold gatherings there while you're away.

Column No 205: March 29, 2009

Assessing House Plans (To Buy or Not to Buy)

It's not uncommon for homebuyers to make a purchase based on the blueprint of a proposed apartment. However, this is not ideal as there is no guarantee the paperwork will give an accurate picture of the final unit. Those buying a flat in an area they are not familiar with won't have any concept of the building's surroundings - and no amount of online satellite imagery can rectify that.

Nonetheless, there are ways to avoid making an unwise choice. When looking at the plans, consider the overall shape of the unit and its rooms. If the shape is too irregular, for example, it has triangular rooms or many acute corners, then it is not a good option. Rectangular and square units with uniform rooms are preferable.

Note the position of the front door; is there a direct line between it and a window, balcony or bedroom door? If so, say no.

If there are bathrooms attached to the bedrooms, does the door to the en-suite open facing the bed position? Will the bedroom doors directly face each other? Will the wall against which you place your bed have a stove or toilet on the other side?

If the answer to any of the above is yes, there are feng shui violations that are best avoided and correcting them may require significant effort.

Column No 208: April 19, 2009

East, West (In the Right Direction)

The Eight Mansions School of feng shui places each individual according to their *kua* or trigram (from the *I Ching*, or *Book of Changes*) number into one of two groups: the east and the west. Calculations are derived from the person's year of birth and not the month, day or hour.

There is also some division based on one's gender but there are certain years when both men and women will have the same number and consequently be in the same group.

Those belonging to the east group have the east, north, south and southeast as their best directions, while those from the west group should orient themselves towards the west, northwest, southwest or northeast whenever possible.

While this school of feng shui has its adherents, general perspective can be lost if one focuses only on making use of preferable directions without taking into account the overall environment; for instance, it is pointless to face a beneficial direction at work if it means sitting with your back to the door. Similarly, if your head being in a favourable direction when you sleep means there is a toilet right behind you, the benefits of the orientation are negated.

If you are in the east group, you should not insist on living in the eastern or southern part of your country or city. There are more complex non-feng shui issues to take into account when determining where to live; feng shui is simply a portion of the entire picture.

Column No 210: May 3, 2009

North, South (The Sense of Direction)

Ancient Chinese cities were built on a north-south, east-west grid. Streets were named according to the direction in which they ran. Houses were built with their backs to the north and their entrances facing south, thereby avoiding the cold winter winds and ensuring that the warmth from the southern sun was received.

In modern cities, roads are not built in the same manner. Feng Shui is no longer used in the mainland to map the orientation of roads; the Communist Party frowns on feng shui being used overtly as it runs contrary to its preference for hard science. In Singapore, right-wing Christians are against what they consider an outdated, ignorant and superstitious practice. Feng shui may be a factor in road building in Hong Kong – but now, of course, not officially,

In modern cities, roads often radiate out in all directions from the centre or are circular. A city may even be built on an inter-cardinal grid (i.e. sitting southeast and facing northwest), especially if the sea or mountains are in these directions. It would be unreasonable to insist on a house that runs exactly north-south in such a city.

If, for instance, the houses of your neighbours face southeast and you insist on yours facing south, your property will not be in harmony with its surroundings. Feng Shui is not about sticking to rigid directions; the nature of the place where you live should always be considered.

Column No 220: July 12, 2009

Feng Shui Credentials (Spin Masters)

Unlike many trades, there is no universally recognized accreditation for feng shui practitioners, which means clients are susceptible to unscrupulous individuals who lack the adequate knowledge, training and experience. This has given feng shui a poor reputation in recent years. So how does one determine whether a feng shui master is genuine?

Titles are not a good indication because anyone can label themselves a 'master' or even 'grand master'. A certificate of attendance in classes run by a renowned feng shui master is also not adequate because this may have been for a few sessions only. Self-proclaimed practitioners who declare they have learnt the art solely from books also have credibility issues.

A genuine feng shui master will readily tell you who they learned from and also specify the amount of time that they spent being an apprentice to that teacher. The teacher's credentials can then be ascertained through the number of books they have published (in English or Putonghua) or by inquiring through other feng shui practitioners. Thus, a lineage may be established, but beware of those who falsely claim to be from a particular lineage.

Perhaps the best indication of a feng shui master's worth can be gleaned from the client referrals he or she has accumulated. Some successful masters depend solely on word of mouth instead of marketing and advertising.

Column No 254: March 21, 2010

Chapter 2

The Bedroom

The Bedroom

On average, we spend a third of our day (eight hours) sleeping, which is why the position of our bed is so important. In feng shui, the worst possible sleeping position is the 'coffin position', where your bed lies directly opposite the door. This position, with the person's feet pointing towards the door, was the way bodies were laid out after death in ancient China.

Sleeping in this position does not mean tragedy or illness will strike the individual. Rather, because the coffin position leaves you exposed to the energy that rushes into the room whenever the door is opened, one will constantly feel lethargic, even after long hours of sleep. In addition, you will be unsettled and irritable, and rarely stay at home.

If you are sleeping in the coffin position, you should reposition your bed. The ideal position is in the corner which is situated diagonally opposite the bedroom door. There should also be a solid wall behind your headboard, so as to anchor your bed.

If you have no choice but to place your bed under a window, ensure that the window is covered when you sleep, otherwise you will tend to have vivid dreams and restless sleep.

For those with insufficient bedroom space, you can place a piece of furniture (such as a bookcase, chest or chair) as a barrier between the foot of your bed and the door.

Column No 4: March 27, 2005

What Lies Above Your Head (What Lies Above)

Have you ever wondered why you sleep better in some rooms than in others? Or why you wake up during the night from a nightmare in an otherwise comfortable hotel room? The answer may lie in what is above the bed, be it a photo, painting or object.

Take the case of a couple living in a serviced apartment who had a painting of a bustling village market located on the wall above their bed. The husband was constantly away on business. In another case, a single man, who had a disproportionately large picture of an embracing couple right above his head, found himself craving a relationship.

According to feng shui, 'what lies above your head' when you sleep can influence your life. For most of us, the ideal image to have above your headboard or overlooking your bed is of a happy couple or family.

It could be an actual picture of your loved ones or a stylised image that you find attractive and soothing. For those who seek achievement, positive images of career or academic success are appropriate. But should you be concerned about being under *any* influence, a blank wall is best.

Column No 13: May 29, 2005

Yin/Yang Imbalances (Balancing Act)

Have you ever felt unsettled in an apartment with breathtaking views visible from floor to ceiling windows? Or perhaps felt uncomfortable in a dark, windowless room with mood lighting and antique furniture? Essentially, you are reacting to environments that are either excessively yang or yin, which is contrary to the balance sought in feng shui.

Excessively yang environments occur when the percentage of windows to walls exceeds 30 per cent. Those living in such conditions may become anxious, impatient, unsettled and unable to concentrate. Occupants may also experience insomnia and dizziness. One solution would be to keep thick curtains or blinds over the large windows. Lace or sheer materials will not reduce the yang energy entering the apartment. Dark-coloured furnishings and dark decorations dark will also help introduce more yin energy.

Spaces with an excess of yin energy lack natural sunlight, such as when the windows directly face adjacent buildings or the window-to-wall ratio is less than 10 per cent. Occupants living in such conditions can feel sluggish, lethargic and unmotivated. They may also be prone to fatigue and arthritis. Try to increase the amount of natural light by keeping the curtains open at all times or opening more windows. Otherwise, introduce strong overhead lighting or play soothing music. The interior design should be kept bright with vibrant colours.

Column No 16: June 19, 2005

Sleeping with Support (Sleep Tight)

For a good night's sleep, the power position, which lies diagonally opposite the entrance of a bedroom, is the most favourable. This allows you to see who enters your room when you are lying in bed. It is inadvisable to place the bed along the same wall as the door or to lie with one's head behind the door. That position should be used only if the other three walls are unavailable because of the positioning of the wardrobe, en-suite or window, for example. You also should not sleep with your bed in the direct path of the bedroom door because the body part opposite the door will be afflicted. If this is the case, move your bed to another spot, or place a solid screen between the door and your bed.

It is ideal to have a wall behind your head when you are sleeping as because this provides stability. If not, you could end up with headaches and health problems. However, if the wall has a toilet or stove directly behind it, it is best to move your bed elsewhere because you could experience vivid dreams and poor sleep. Sleeping with your head against a window will give you a feeling of insecurity. If this is the only option available, you should hang thick curtains and keep them drawn when you sleep. Thin curtains that allow light to filter through are insufficient. Never underestimate the benefits of a good night's sleep.

Column No 20: July 17, 2005

Types of Beds (Snooze Patrol)

Certain feng shui guidelines govern bed design and structure. For instance, a bed should be an acceptable distance from the floor. Although some feng shui masters believe sleeping on the floor has no adverse effects, a significant number feel this will cause the occupant to absorb the yin energy of the floor, creating health problems such as lethargy and joint stiffness. Having a bed that is too high from the floor imparts a sense of instability that will affect your daily life.

Two mattresses pushed together to form an extra-large bed can pose problems for a couple's love life, suggesting both partners will have separate lives and spend long periods apart. And mattresses that are too short for the occupant not only cause back problems; but the person concerned could encounter professional and personal obstacles. The same principle applies to beds without a headboard, as it denotes a lack of support. This may be compensated for if the bed is against a wall.

The area below one's bed should not be used for storage as this stops the chi underneath from circulating; causing the occupant to feel unsettled and agitated. Removing and disposing of the debris that lies under a bed improves wellbeing and the quality of sleep.

Column No 40: December 4, 2005

Between Two Windows (Middle Ground)

In residential feng shui, the placement of the bed is second only in importance to the position of the front door. When one's bed is positioned between two windows, pillars or doors, there will be health problems. Whichever part of the body lies in the direct path between the doors or structures will be adversely affected. Should the head lie between the two structures, there will be a higher probability of headaches. If it's the abdomen, there will be an increased incidence of gastritis, indigestion and heartburn. Female occupants sleeping in such an exposed and vulnerable position may also find it difficult to fall pregnant.

The rationale behind these problems is that doors or windows opposite another similar structure create a vortex of energy that will traverse across anything that lies in between. Likewise the area between two pillars will be prone to the pressure generated by these opposing columns.

If your bed is situated in such a way, reposition it if you can. If this is not practical, place a screen or hang a curtain over the doors or windows to nullify the effect. With regard to windows, keep the curtains drawn over the one with the less pleasant view. You may also choose to stop using the door by placing a cabinet or chest of drawers in front of it.

Hanging crystals to create a cushion between a structure and your bed will have little effect.

Column No 41: December 11, 2005

Bedroom Location (Pillow Talk)

Bedrooms are our personal rest areas and there are guidelines when it comes to their location relative to each other and to other areas in the home. Bedrooms should not be next to the front door, or too far from other bedrooms, as this suggests their occupants have separate lives from the other members of the household.

The doors of bedrooms accessed via a common corridor should not be directly opposite each other. If they are, both bedrooms compete for the same energy, resulting in conflicts between their occupants. Some feng shui masters use mirrors or even hang curtains over bedroom doors to alleviate these problems. Ideally, there should be a wall directly opposite a bedroom door.

Should the door to a bedroom be situated at the end of a long corridor, ensure the bed is definitely not in the path of the door, otherwise the occupants may suffer health problems such as headaches and insomnia.

Bedroom doors should also not be directly opposite kitchen or toilet doors as the energy from these areas will enter the room, causing its occupants to feel unsettled. A bedroom next to a kitchen or toilet is not a problem as long as the head of the bed does not abut the same wall as a cooker or toilet.

Column No 89: November 26, 2006

Romance Sectors (In the Mood for Love)

In the quest for love, several formulas are used to calculate the romance sector. Some use your personal astrological data; others take into account annual influences in your living space. The Flying Stars School identifies a different one of the eight directions as the romance sector each year.

To stimulate one's love life, some masters advocate the placement of a water feature or vase of flowers in this sector while others suggest installing an aquarium, with a specific number of fish determined by your year of birth. A water feature ideally should not be placed in the bedroom; if this is unavoidable, ensure it is switched off while you sleep. It should be kept clean and should not be allowed to run dry.

In classical feng shui, the southwest sector is not always associated with romance, so placing a pair of mandarin ducks or the double happiness symbol in this sector of your home will do little to enhance your romantic prospects.

Moreover, feng shui works in tandem with destiny and personal effort, which means interventions can only achieve so much if there are other issues (such as a person's expectations of relationships) that need to be addressed first.

Column No 105: April 1, 2007

Televisions in Bedrooms (Electric Blues)

There has been much debate as to whether the presence of televisions in bedrooms contravenes feng shui principles. Some consultants refuse to comment on the issue except to say that such modern equipment is not mentioned in classical texts. This is unhelpful because feng shui is the art of living in harmony with your environment and therefore it has to incorporate aspects of modern life.

Having electrical equipment inside a yin environment will cause the occupant to feel restless and irritable because of the amount of yang energy that is generated. Occupants may suffer from insomnia or feel fatigued, even after many hours of sleep. This is especially true if you sleep with a computer and monitor left on in the bedroom.

However, some people find watching TV lulls them to sleep. If you are one of them, ensure that the TV is on a timer that turns it off after a certain period has elapsed.

The screen should not be too big or too close to the viewer and should be covered if you can clearly see your reflection in it when lying in bed and the set is off. Undoubtedly the best approach is to remove all electrical equipment from your bedroom. You will be surprised by how soundly you sleep after that.

Column No 145: January 13, 2008

Relationship Problems (Positioned for Peace)

If, after moving into a new home, personal relationships within your family deteriorate, check the following feng shui issues.

Are there any mirrors in the bedroom that reflect the occupants when they sleep? If so, you should remove them, or cover the reflections. This includes mirrors on dressing tables that face the bed or wardrobes with mirrored doors. Are there exposed beams above where you sleep?

Watch out for those above the middle of the bed, including structural protrusions that contain air conditioning ducts.

Cover the beams with a false ceiling or reposition the bed. Are there any unsettling, turbulent or melancholic images on display? These can include scenes of waterfalls, storms or savage animals, and abstract art involving dark and moody colours or lonely figures. Do bedroom doors face each other? If so, cover at least one with curtains.

In the kitchen, are the water and fire elements, such as the sink and stove, directly opposite each other? They shouldn't be. If you can't relocate the stove, place a green or wooden mat in between the two.

Column No 194: January 4, 2009

Health Problems (Bed Rests)

If you are suffering from health problems, feng shui issues could be to blame.

Start looking for the cause in your bedroom. If you suffer from headaches and/or insomnia, ensure your bed has a solid headboard and is not in the centre of the room. Make sure the bed is not flush against a wall with windows. If it is, move it or put up curtains that are drawn when you sleep. Mirrors opposite your bed should be moved or covered, even if you can't see your reflection when you are lying down.

There should be no plants or aquariums in your bedroom. If the wealth sector of the home lies in the bedroom and you have brought in a water fountain to take advantage of the fact, switch it off while you sleep.

If problems involve specific parts of the body, such as the neck, elbow or knee, ensure your bed is not side on to the door of the en suite bathroom. If the bed cannot be moved, place a screen or some furniture between the door and the bed.

Alternatively, you can also place thick curtains on the inside of the door and keep them drawn when you are asleep. Check for lighting or ceiling fans above the affected part of your body. If you can, reposition your bed or remove these structures.

Column No 195: January 11, 2009

Moving Rooms (En Suite Dreams)

The room that you are using as a bedroom may not be the best for you, and sleeping in your study or guest room may be better from a feng shui perspective.

There could be several reasons for this. If the room looks onto a disruptive structure with significant cutting or *sha* energy, such as a bridge or construction site, it would be wise to move into a room that will provide you with more calm and tranquility.

If there is an en-suite in the room, note the position of the toilet door relative to your bed: is any part of your body in a direct line from the door? Are your feet pointing to the door when you are lying in bed?

If you experience physical problems in the body parts that line up with the toilet door while you sleep – such as headaches, knee problems, digestion issues - then it is recommended that you move to a room with no bathroom attached.

As always, though, you need to take into account your own needs and requirements.

Column No 214: May 31, 2009

Sleeping Positions (Look before You Sleep)

The direction in which your head points while you sleep undeniably plays a role in your well-being, believe feng shui masters, but what is more important is that you ensure your head rests against a solid frame, which may be made of wood or metal.

Without such backing, you may feel insecure or unsupported in your personal and/or professional lives. You may discover that colleagues and acquaintances have been criticizing you without you being fully aware of the fact.

Do not be tempted to sleep with your head pointing towards the foot of the bed, even if you have read, or heard from a friend, that someone of your year of birth should sleep in a specific direction. Tangible influences will always have more effect than those that are less obvious, such as orientation.

Ideally, both types of influence should be combined to form the optimal sleeping position. But what may have worked well for a friend in his living space may not be as effective for you, as different homes have different attributes.

Column No 225: August 16, 2009

Chapter 3

Children and Pregnancy

Study (A Desk Job)

As both the workplace and school become more demanding and competitive, we need an area at home where we can work. Even with limited space, it would be unwise to be working on your laptop when lying in bed, because the bedroom is a personal area that should be kept separate from work. However, parents often place a desk in their children's bedrooms so they can do their homework there.

Ideally, the study area should be a separate room that can accommodate a computer, fax machine etc. Ensure that you sit facing the door with your back against a solid wall. Sitting with your back to the door or the window will give you a feeling of instability. Should you face the window when you work, your concentration will be affected. If there is no choice but to have your back to a window, ensure that the curtains are drawn when you are working.

These principles also apply to desks in children's rooms. One of the common mistakes I have observed is that the child sits with his back to the door with shelves positioned directly overhead. Reorient the desk and there should be a significant change.

There are also specific formulas to determine the academic sector for the person's birth year, as well as the current year sector (known in Cantonese as *mun cheong wai*).

Column No 9: May 1, 2005

Children's Room (Little Decisions)

With the tendency for smaller families, it is common for children to have their own bedroom rather than share it with siblings. Certain feng shui guidelines should be considered with regard to the entrance of a child's room. Ideally, their door should not be opposite that of their parents, otherwise conflicts could arise. To minimise health problems, a child's bedroom door should not be opposite the door to a toilet.

The general principles of all bedrooms apply to the interior of children's rooms: they should sleep with a wall behind their heads for support and not in the path of the door. Cribs should not be left 'floating' in the centre of the room. For young children, there should not be any toys present that are significantly larger than them, as this may overwhelm them.

There should also not be any threatening or disturbing pictures, particularly of tigers and other wild animals or images of violence and war, as this will interfere with their sleep.

For older children, a desk should be placed so they either face the door or are able to see who enters. Sitting with their backs to the entrance will impair their concentration. It's best not to have electrical equipment such as televisions in the bedroom because they are excessively yang and could unsettle or agitate a child.

Column No 18: July 3, 2005

Pregnancy (Mother Care)

When it comes to pregnancy and conception, there are a number of feng shui principles that should be followed to ensure the health of mother and baby.

Your sleeping position is extremely important for conception. There should be no sharp structures (trees, roofs of neighbouring houses, edges of buildings) pointing towards your bed, while there should not be anything hanging above you, such as fans or lights, especially over the lower abdomen. Preferably, the toilet or bedroom door should not open towards your body. Any of these 'violations' will lead to difficulties with conception.

If you are already pregnant, try to delay any renovation work involving hammering, drilling or knocking. If the work cannot be postponed, ensure you are not at home while it is being carried out.

This also applies to moving furniture because it is possible to scratch and chip the walls. The Chinese believe that the spirit of the foetus is already present in the house and any damage to the walls or ceiling of your home will result in injury to the unborn child.

Also, you should not change the position of your bed when you are pregnant, otherwise the instability generated will adversely affect the pregnancy. This explains why some families are reluctant to move house until a child is born.

Column No 35: October 30, 2005

Double Decker Beds (Double Trouble)

In an attempt to make better use of their living space, parents may consider purchasing double-deck, or bunk beds for their children. These beds come in a variety of designs.

While children may find the double-decker approach novel and fun, some feng shui masters feel that such sleeping arrangements contravene some of their principles.

The child sleeping on the lower bed is under the constant pressure exerted by the structure above, while the child sleeping above on top is extremely close to the ceiling and may be unable to fully extend his or her body while sitting. Both children will thus encounter obstacles in terms of health and study.

In T shaped bunk-bed units, parts of the body of the person sleeping on the lower level may be adversely affected. This is because the sharp edge of the bed above will press down on the body below.

Similarly, children attempting to study at a desk located under their bed will tend to have a higher incidence of headaches and may suffer from poor concentration.

If there is only one person using a bunk-bed, it is inadvisable to use the unslept-in space as a storage area.

Column No 43: January 1, 2006

Nursery (Child's Play)

The same feng shui principles governing the position of a bed in a bedroom also apply to the placement of a baby's cot in a nursery. For instance, the cot should not be placed directly opposite the door with the feet pointing outside, as this exposes the baby to the incoming energy whenever the door is open, resulting in poor sleep.

No part of the cot should be in the path of the nursery or toilet doors, or the associated body part will be adversely affected. (If the middle of the cot is in the path of the nursery door, then the baby will be prone to stomach problems.) Ideally, the cot should be placed against a wall for solid backing, and not in the centre of the room, where it lacks support.

The cot should also not be placed under beams, ceiling edges or overhanging structures such as lights, overhead fans or air conditioning units. It should be in the sector of the room where the ceiling is highest, as placing it under the lowest part may affect the physical growth of your child.

The nursery should preferably have soft and neutral colours such as cream and beige, because extremely yang colours such as red will make it hard for the baby to settle. Painting the walls with excessively yin colours such as black and blue is also not recommended, as it does not foster the growth of your child.

Column No 100: February 25, 2007

Academic Studies (Live and Learn)

Students wanting to improve their results should enhance the *mun cheong wai*, or academic sector, this year. There are two main formulas to identifying this sector. As per the Flying Stars school, the academic sector is associated with the presence of the 1-White water star. Its location can be found in any Chinese almanac, and changes every year.

The Three Harmony (*San He*) method derives the sector from the element of the year. For example, in a yin fire year, the academic sector will be in the southwest. Traditionally, symbols of scholarly achievement, such as an inkstand with brushes, should be placed in this sector to improve results.

You may also position your desk in the academic area to stimulate your focus. The desk should ideally be placed so you sit with your back to a wall and face the entrance to your room or study without being in its direct path. Sitting with your back to the door may impair concentration, as will facing a window, especially one with a view.

It's best to have the window to your left or right, so you can receive natural sunlight without your attention wavering. There should not be any cabinets, shelves or structures such as lights or fans above your head while you study.

Column No 104: March 25, 2007

Newborn Celebrations (Baby Talk)

Chinese tradition dictates that a newborn baby is seen by relatives and friends only after he or she has been in the world for a full month, allowing the child to build up immunity against infections. Traditionally, new mothers were also confined to the home and fed a strict diet of steamed meat and vegetables to help them regain strength.

During the first week after a baby's birth, parents can consult a feng shui master to help decide upon a name. From the time of birth, the master will be able to determine which elements, and therefore which characters, will bring balance and harmony to the newborn's Chinese name.

For the first month celebration, guests bestow gifts such as baby clothes, shoes, caps and gold and silver jewellery. Red *lai see* packets can also be given as part of the celebrations. The newborn should be dressed in red to greet the guests and will also have a gold or silver padlock on a red string hung around the neck to anchor him or her to the world.

Red eggs being a symbol of life and energy are given to guests to mark the happy occasion. Traditionally, a child's head will be shaved on their 29th day in readiness for the full-month celebration.

Column No 234: October 18, 2009

Chapter 4

Colours, Numbers and Water

Water Features (Water Works)

There's a common misconception that the larger the water feature (such as aquariums or fountains), the more wealth it will bring. Which may explain why I have seen gigantic aquariums filled with fish in some bedrooms. Unfortunately, not only did these water features fail to increase wealth, the person with the bedroom aquarium bedroom always had money problems. So what is the actual role of water features in feng shui?

They are used to stimulate the wealth sector in one's home. In Hong Kong where there are often space constraints, this may take the form of an electrically operated rotating marble ball or a fish tank with a filter. There are various ways to calculate where water should be located within a home, with each feng shui school advocating its own formula.

I advise against untrained individuals carrying out these calculations. What's more important are the general principles: the water feature should be proportional in size to the room, it should be kept clean and the water never allowed to evaporate completely.

One should also maintain perspective. If a feng shui master tells you to fill a bowl with water and place it in a certain spot, repeating the task each morning, be aware of the inconvenience it causes and question its validity. Feng Shui is meant to enhance one's life, not create additional stress.

Column No 11: May 15, 2005

The Colour Red (Red Alert)

Red is considered an auspicious colour in Chinese culture because it represents happiness and good fortune. During the Lunar New Year holiday, gift money is enclosed in red packets, scrolls are written on red paper and many people wear red when visiting family and friends.

Red symbolises fire, which is extremely yang in nature. It would be unwise to paint the walls and ceilings of your home and bedroom entirely red because this would cause an excess of yang energy, which can result in irritability, headaches and poor sleep. Some feng shui practitioners believe the overuse of red also stimulates the negative earth energy that is present in certain sectors, leading to mishaps and accidents.

Painting your kitchen red, for example, could increase the risk of fire. A professional feng shui consultant should assess your property before advising on the amount of red that can be used and where. Unlike in domestic situations, red walls and carpets are recommended for a restaurant because the yang energy stimulates businesses.

It's also unwise to wear red all the time. Chinese astrologers usually consider a person's time of birth when determining which of the five elements is suitable for them. If fire is inappropriate, a wearer of red will feel drained and agitated if they chose to don no other colour.

Column No 47: February 5, 2006

Numbers (Part 1 - Magic Numbers)

It is not unusual to see luxury cars with number plates featuring '888' on Hong Kong roads. In contrast, one would be hard-pressed to find floors ending with the number four, even in new skyscrapers. Instead, the sequence of floors will go from the third to the fifth, skipping the inauspicious level.

There are cultural and linguistic factors why certain numbers are considered auspicious and others are to be avoided at all costs.

Number one suggests immediacy; it hastens and amplifies the effects of the numbers that follow. In feng shui, one represents academic achievement and romance. In Cantonese, the word for two sounds the same as 'ease'. When a combination of numbers starts with two, the symbolism of the numbers that follows will be easily achieved. However, the implication of two in classical feng shui is bleak; it is the number of illness and poor health.

Phonetically, three sounds the same as 'birth' in Cantonese. It symbolises new beginnings and is considered auspicious. In feng shui, three implies activity and initiative that may result in aggression if left unchecked.

Column No 48: February 12, 2006

Numbers (Part 2 - Figure Conscious)

The word for 'four' in Cantonese sounds like the word 'death'. As a result, it strikes fear into Cantonese speakers and is a number to be avoided. When paired with other numbers, its negative implications can be magnified. For example, 24 sounds like 'ease of death'. However, some feng shui masters view four as the number for academic achievement and romance, and advise clients not to fear it.

The word for 'five' in Cantonese sounds the same as 'lacking' or 'without', so when paired with four it can negate the association with death. For instance, 54 suggests an enterprise will never wither or die. But in Classical feng shui, five is the most negative number and is avoided.

The word for 'six' rhymes with road and, when put with other numbers, implies one is on the path to success or calamity. Feng Shui masters view six as a number of authority. There is no major cultural significance associated with the number seven and in Classical feng shui it is viewed both positively (communication) and negatively (robbery).

Auspicious 'eight' sounds the same as 'good fortune' and 'wealth' in Cantonese, which explains why it is highly sought after. Two eights together double the good luck and three treble it. Fortuitously, we are now in a 20-year feng shui cycle in which eight is the number of prosperity.

Column No 49: February 19, 2006

Numbers (Part 3 - Safe Combinations)

The number nine suggests a sense of completion or sufficiency – the idea that one will have enough. Depending on the numbers that follow, this can either be auspicious or inauspicious. Classical feng shui masters view nine as the number of celebrations but are aware that it also represents fire, with an excess of it resulting in fire outbreaks.

Having examined this basic feng shui numerology, the significance behind certain combinations can be seen. Thirty-four suggests birth followed by loss, 44 would be double death, 64 the road to demise and 84 good fortune followed by catastrophe. Conversely, 168 means that one would be on the road to success, 368 denotes that one would be born on the road of success and 128 implies that one will easily attain wealth and good fortune.

The dreaded 444 triples the probability of demise while the highly sought after 888 triples one's happiness and luck. However, the number preceding the subsequent number can bring about the opposite effect: while 54 denotes one will not sustain any losses, 58 implies one will have not any good luck.

Perhaps the best way to circumnavigate the minefield of Chinese numerological combinations is to have a native Cantonese speaker close at hand.

Column No 50: February 26, 2007

Aquariums (Fishy Business)

The practice of keeping aquariums is not limited to fans of tropical fish. Some feng shui masters recommend the placement of aquariums to stimulate wealth and elevate prospects. In Classical feng shui, water represents wealth and moving water is believed to stimulate the wealth energy in your environment. Having an aquarium with fish and an oxygen pump will result in constantly moving water, thereby magnifying the wealth energy.

Water should always be kept clean and fresh – dirty or stagnant water will adversely affect your prospects. The size of the aquarium should also be proportional to the size of the room: having a small fish bowl in a large living room will not yield much benefit, and vice versa. An aquarium should never be placed in a bedroom, as its yang energy will interfere with the room's yin energy.

You may also need professional advice to correctly identify your wealth sector.

Feng Shui masters will use your year of birth to advise you on the number of fish you should keep in your aquarium. There is no necessity to keep large or expensive species of fish such as koi or arrowana if you have space or budget constraints. Fish that have died in the aquarium should be replaced.

Column No 120: July 15, 2007

Use of Colours (Colour Me Beautiful)

Feng Shui masters who take into account aspects of modern living know the colour of the walls in a home has an effect on its occupants. For instance, it is not recommended to paint the northern sector of your home (water direction) bright red because the colour (representing the fire element) will clash. Red may also stimulate the troublesome 'Five-Yellow' earth energy.

Red is extremely yang, which is why it should not be used for yin areas, such as bedrooms, otherwise occupants will experience sleeping difficulties. Using red for the study may result in concentration problems. While red can be used in yang sectors such as the living and dining rooms, excessive use will cause occupants to feel irritable, resulting in arguments. Painting a feature wall is acceptable but calculations involving the orientation of the property and location of the room need to be taken into account.

In contrast, the colours black and blue, which represent water, are extremely yin; excessive use of them may cause occupants to feel lethargic. For instance, you should not paint the walls and the ceiling of your child's bedroom black to simulate the night sky, otherwise he or she may feel drained. The water element also represents romance and using black and blue may cause romantic complications.

Column No 155: March 30, 2008

Use of Colours 2 (Colour Scheming)

When determining which colours are suitable for your home, feng shui consultants take into account factors such as the orientation and age of your property, the location of each room relative to the centre, and also the astrological data of the occupants. From the time of a person's birth, a consultant can calculate which elements are favourable. The use of colours that clash with the occupant will have undesirable consequences.

Neutral earth colours such as beige and cream are not excessively yin or yang and are therefore able to bring balance to a room. White is not considered too stark and represents metal, which may not be suitable for some, resulting in an increased incidence of accidents.

Green represents wood and is too strong to be used for more than one wall. It may also cause digestive or reproductive problems for the occupants.

Another way of utilising colours is through the use of soft furnishings or artwork. For instance, to stimulate romance, introduce water and wood elements through the use of light blue curtains and images of a green field or forest. Black also represents water but it is usually not recommended due to its association with death.

Column No 156: April 6, 2008

Water (Streams of Consciousness)

Having water in front of your residence is considered ideal in feng shui terms, which would help explain why you may have seen water fountains in front of homes. However, the quality and flow of the water should also be taken into account. Living near a storm drain containing stagnant water or sewerage is not recommended and a seaside home by a stretch of water that is always choppy will unsettle or agitate occupants. It is preferable to have an ocean-front building facing a sheltered cove with calm water.

It is wise to ensure that water does not dominate the structure. Note also the formation of the water. A property located inside the bend of a river would be a far better home than one positioned against the outside edge or curve of the bend. In traditional feng shui terms, those within the bend are being embraced or protected, while those at the outer edge are considered to be in opposition.

There are classical water formulas that can be used to determine the effects of surrounding water on a property and they include Dragon Gate, Three Harmony and Nine Stars methods. However, these formulas should be used only to assist you in finding an environment where these water patterns occur naturally. Spending considerable amounts of money on drains around your home to simulate these water formulas is ineffective and potentially damaging.

Column No 191: December 7, 2008

Red (Colour Co-ordination)

During the festive season, Hong Kong is decked out in red as it is believed the colour attracts prosperity in the New Year. While there's no doubt that red represents good fortune and auspiciousness, it is also an extremely yang colour, meaning that it may not be suitable for all.

Astrologers measure the strength of the five elements (water, wood, fire, metal and earth) at your time of birth to determine not only your personality, health, familial background and marriage prospects, but also your fortune and luck at certain stages of your life. For those who require the fire element to strengthen or balance their fortune, the colour red is recommended. It is appropriate for such individuals to wear red for important meetings and appointments, to drive a red car and to use red linen and soft furnishings. They might find that the addition of red gives them extra confidence and self-assurance.

However, the colour is not recommended for those whose chart contains excessive fire already. When such people wear red, they are likely to feel agitated, irritated or stifled and may become easily exhausted. For them, driving a red car could be dangerous.

Before deciding on new clothes or a car, then, it may be wise to consult an experienced astrologer to find out how 'fiery' your chart is. Don't assume red is beneficial for everyone.

Column No 198: February 8, 2009

Unlucky Floors (Another Storey)

You may have noticed that certain floors in an apartment building are 'missing'; often there are no fourth, 14th, 24th, 34th floor, etc. in predominantly Chinese areas. This is because 'four' sounds like the word 'death' in Cantonese, making it unpopular with both tenants and landlords, who will also often number an apartment 3A to avoid using the unlucky number. Some buildings have no 13th floor (as per Western tradition), making the floor after the 12th the 15th.

The concern over the number four is cultural rather than related to metaphysical calculations, and some traditional feng shui masters deride it as superstition.

In the Flying Stars School of feng shui, the number four is instead associated with romance and academic studies. The negative numbers in that system are two and five, the former associated with illness and the latter with catastrophes. Indeed, there are a few buildings that as well as not having the fourth floor, also omit the second and fifth, which means the second floor is known as the third and the sixth is only three levels above the ground floor.

The cultural beliefs associated with the number four are so deeply entwined that even phone numbers or car registration plates that feature it are generally avoided. Perhaps the best advice for those wary of the number four is to write off the fear as irrational.

Column No 229: September 13, 2009

Chapter 5

Date Selection

Choosing a Good Day (Day By Day)

Have you noticed how on certain days there are long queues outside Hong Kong marriage registry centres, while banquet halls and restaurants are booked out for wedding celebrations? These circumstances can be attributed to the Chinese almanac, which stipulates good and bad days for undertaking certain activities. In feng shui, timing is paramount, because carrying out modifications on inauspicious days may nullify or reduce their potential benefits.

The almanac is essentially a tabulation of the Chinese solar and lunar calendars and provides information on the elements and Chinese zodiac animals that govern specific days. Various systems are used to determine the auspiciousness of a certain day, the two main ones being astronomical (the cycle of the 28 lunar constellations) and astrological (the time, day, month and year of birth of the individuals involved).

A wide range of auspicious/inauspicious activities are covered in the almanac, such as engagements, weddings, signing of contracts, moving into new apartments or offices, opening new businesses, moving your bed, traveling and even cutting your hair.

Previously published only in Chinese, there are numerous English translations of the almanac now available, so don't miss out on the benefits of date selection.

Column No 26: August 28, 2005

Renovations (Building Tension)

If you carry out renovations, there are three areas you should be wary of, the first being the Grand Duke Jupiter or Tai Sui sector, which, in each annual cycle, falls in a different sector. This is the direction represented by the zodiac animal of the current year.

The next sector to be aware of is the Clash sector, which is the area occupied by the zodiac animal that directly opposes the Grand Duke. For the Year of the Dog, for example, the Clash animal is the Dragon, which is associated with the southeast.

Finally, the Three *Shars* or Three Conflicts direction should also be noted. This direction belongs to the element that conflicts with the element of the current year. So in this example, the dog is associated with the fire element, which clashes with water, represented by the north. So the Three *Shars* are in the north.

A Chinese Almanac is necessary to identify these directions for a specific year.

In the event that significant work (for example, drilling or digging) is carried out in any of these sectors of your property, there may be an increased incidence of accidents, mishaps and illness for the occupants. To rectify this situation, start from a neutral sector and work towards the problematic one. If you need to renovate the southeast this year, for instance, you can start in either the east or south then work your way towards the Clash sector.

Column No 52: March 12, 2006

69

Using the Chinese Almanac 1 (By the Book)

The traditional Chinese almanac that details auspicious and inauspicious activities for each day of the year has now been translated into English and is widely available in Hong Kong, and many other Chinatown bookshops. The amount of information provided for each day may differ from one edition to another, but all of them will state the western calendar date and its representation via an element and an animal sign (for example, March 19, 2006: fire goat). Some may also add the lunar equivalent.

The 12 zodiac animals, also known as the 12 earthly or terrestrial branches, do not just represent years: they are also used to symbolise 12 months, days and even 12 double-hours. By knowing the animal sign of the day, the reader will be able to identify the clashing sign; the animal that lies directly opposite in the zodiac cycle.

Therefore, the day of the goat may not be a good one for those born in the year of the ox, as the ox clashes with the goat.

Each animal sign has an associated element, which can also signify another form of trouble. Referring to the cycle of the five elements, a fire day, for example, will be problematic for those born on a metal day. Hence, the fire goat day March 19 could be difficult for those born in the metal ox year 1961, especially if they are getting married or are moving house.

Column No 53: March 19, 2006

Using the Almanac 2 (Little Red Books)

Not only does the Chinese almanac indicate the suitability of a day for individuals, but it also mentions which type of activities are favourable or unfavourable for that day. For instance, March 26, 2006 was a good day for signing contracts or opening a new business, but a bad day for religious activity or opening a warehouse. Auspicious periods of the day are also identified.

The Duty Cycle of the day is also mentioned, which is related to the activity of the lunar constellations. For March 26, 2006 for example, the ruler is 'Close', which is favourable. Other information from different schools of feng shui may also be provided, depending on the edition you purchased.

Some almanacs state that the Three *Shars* or Three Conflicts direction is not an auspicious direction. For example, if on a specific date the Three *Shars* lay in the north, it will therefore not be advisable to carry out renovations in the north, or even to move one's bed towards the north on that day. The Three Conflicts direction is derived from the *San He* (Three Combinations or Harmony) school, which emphasises astrological data.

The Flying Stars School's calculations may also be included in the Almanac. For example, if that year's Flying Star is the Three Jade Star, which means the Five-Yellow Star flies into the west, it thereby making the west unsuitable for activities like digging or construction. A feng shui professional can advise you on the benefits and restrictions of each traditional school of feng shui.

Column No 54: March 26, 2006

Renovations (In a Fix)

The Grand Duke Jupiter sector, or Tai Sui, is the direction represented by the Chinese zodiac animal of the year. For example, there are several sectors to avoid if you are doing renovations in the Year of the Pig. The direction associated with the Pig lies in the northwest, or specifically, from about 322 to 338 degrees. Carrying out renovations such as drilling or hammering in this sector, in that year, may exacerbate pre-existing health problems.

There is however no need to move out, or hang wind chimes over your front door, if your home faces this direction. Simply ensure no renovations or extensions are carried out in this sector for the rest of the year.

Don't be concerned if you sit with your back to the Grand Duke in your office. If you face the Grand Duke, however, you should change your position.

The next sector to consider is the Clash or Year Breaker Sector, which is represented by the animal that is in opposition to the animal of the year. In 2007, for example, it is the sector represented by the Snake, which is associated with the southeast, from 142 to 158 degrees. Carrying out repairs or renovations in this sector will aggravate health problems and conflicts between occupants. If renovations are unavoidable in these sectors, an experienced feng shui consultant should be able to advise on specific dates to start work, thereby minimising any adverse effects.

Column No 102: March 11, 2007

More Renovations (Building Pressure)

As well as the Grand Duke and the Clash sectors, you should avoid carrying out renovations in the Three Afflictions, or Three *Shars*, sector. This is the direction that corresponds to the element in conflict with the element of the current year.

The Pig is associated with wood, which clashes with metal, represented by the west. Construction work in this sector will create problems ranging from increased incidence of accidents and burglary, to the ill-health of the occupants. If you regularly sit, at home or in the office, either facing or with your back to this sector, no problems should arise. Also, there's no need place any objects in this sector to neutralize negative energy.

If the negative Five-Yellow Earth Star, which contains negative energy associated with mishaps and disasters, is in the northeast sector, for example, then drilling holes or knocking down walls here will badly affect both health and wealth.

Some feng shui masters recommend placing coins or metal wind chimes in this sector to reduce the negative earth energy. If renovations are unavoidable in this area, an experienced feng shui consultant should advise on favourable times to start work.

Alternatively, you can work from a neutral sector towards an afflicted one to minimise negative consequences.

Column No 103: March 18, 2007

Grand Duke Jupiter (Calming Spirits)

You may have come across Tai Sui in television or radio programmes or magazine articles that deal with feng shui and astrological predictions. Essentially, Tai Sui refers to the celestial spirit that presides over the year. It is also known as the Grand Duke Jupiter, as it is believed to correspond to the 60-year cycle of the planet Jupiter rotating around the sun. In temples dedicated to the presiding year god, the entire pantheon of the 60 celestial year spirits can be found in a row of miniature figures.

In 2008 for example, those born in the years of the Rat (including 1948, 1960, 1972, 1984, or 2008) will offend Tai Sui while those born in the years of the Horse (1954, 1966 and 1978, for example) will clash with it. Those who either offend or clash with the presiding god of the year should make offerings to it, to avert any potential catastrophes in the year to follow.

Tai Sui corresponds to the ruling zodiac animal of the year. Each animal occupies a 15-degree sector. For the Year of the Rat, for example, the Tai Sui sector lies in the north and runs from 352.5 to 7.5 degrees.

Feng Shui masters will warn against carrying out major renovations in this sector as they will stimulate negative energy, resulting in health issues, arguments and burglaries. Those people who face Tai Sui while at their desks are advised to modify their positions.

Column No 150: February 24, 2008

Chinese Months (Dating Game)

The 12 animals of the Chinese zodiac represent not only years but also months, days and hours. Each of the 12 animals roughly corresponds to one month in the western calendar.

For example, May is the month of the Snake while June is that of the Horse. However, rather than starting on May 1 and ending on May 31, the Snake month starts on May 5 and runs until June 4, plus or minus a day or so.

Another difference between the two calendars is that the first month of the Chinese solar calendar is usually considered to be February, which marks the start of spring. The animal associated with spring is the tiger, the third animal of the Chinese zodiac.

The animals follow their familiar order, so March is the month of the rabbit, the fourth animal of the zodiac and so on. December is thus the month of the Rat and January that of the Ox.

The start of each month corresponds to a seasonal event that is marked by specific activities. Ching Ming, for instance, the festival for ancestor worship and tomb-sweeping, falls on the first day of the second, or rabbit, month, April 5. The animal months are also used for guidance in choosing auspicious dates for weddings and opening businesses.

Column No 163: May 25, 2008

Days and Hours (Time Management)

You may have read that the 12 Chinese zodiac animals are each combined with one of the five elements (wood, fire, earth, metal or water) to form the sexagenary (60-fold) cycle to denote years. For instance, 2007 was the Year of the Fire Pig, while 2008 was the Year of the Earth Rat. This sequence of 60 elements combined with animals is also used to measure months, days and hours. (For example, June 1, 2008 was the Day of the Water Monkey).

To find out the element-animal combination for a specific date, a traditional Chinese calendar is needed. This information is then used for date-selection purposes: those born in the Year of the Tiger (for example, 1950, 1962, 1974, 1986 and 1998) are advised not to carry out any significant activities on that day.

Traditionally, the Chinese view time in two-hour units or double-hours. As there are 24 hours in a day, there are 12 units, with each unit corresponding to one of the 12 animals. The double-hour of the Rat runs from 11pm the previous day to 1am the current day, followed by the Ox hour from 1am to 3am. The remaining animals then follow in their familiar sequence, with the Pig Hour running from 9pm to 11pm.

Some feng shui masters, therefore, state that the day starts at 11pm and ends an hour earlier than the western day.

Column No 164: June 1, 2008

Date Selection (Perfect Timing)

When feng shui masters consult, not only do they take into account the physical changes that need to be undertaken, such as moving furniture around, but also the time in which they are to be done. Date selection is based on the philosophy that time is cyclical; positive and negative occasions occur throughout one's life at intervals that can be specified through analysing one's birth data.

The Chinese use the 10 Heavenly Stems (or the five elements in their yang and yin forms) and the 12 Earthly Branches (the 12 animals of the zodiac) matched together to quantify time, in four units: year, month, day and hour.

To choose an auspicious time to carry out a specific activity, such as a wedding, or a move to a new home, all four units of time have to be balanced and conducive to the person's year of birth and, if there is an office or residence involved, the orientation of the property.

The *Tong Shu* or Chinese almanac contains all the information that has been collated by Chinese astronomers and astrologers and is an essential tool for such date selection. In Hong Kong, it is known as the *Tong Seng*, as *shu*, which means 'book' in Putonghua, sounds like 'loss' in Cantonese. In contrast, *seng* means 'win' or 'victory', an apparently far more auspicious connotation.

Column 215: June 7, 2009

Chinese Almanac (Formula for Success)

The Chinese almanac not only contains information about what activities should be performed on specific days, it also has data on topics ranging from palmistry and face reading to water formulas and the position of stars. The almanac is usually published in late autumn, long before the end of the western calendar year.

Previously only available in Putonghua, over the last decade, English translations - which usually contain the general astrological forecasts for each of the 12 zodiac animals signs – have been made available.

More detailed astrological forecasts specific to the five types of zodiac animal - the water, wood, fire, earth and metal variations – are also published, both in print and online. These forecasts contain 60 sections, one for each of the element-animal combinations. Those born in 1949 and 2009 belong to the *earth* oxen group, for instance, and those born in 1997 are *fire* oxen.

General feng shui information specific to the year is also mentioned in the Chinese almanac. Positive sectors, such as the wealth, academic and romance areas, are identified; and negative sectors, such as those that result in health problems or accidents if, for instance, renovations are carried out, are also pinpointed. Although the technical jargon in the almanac can often be confusing to the casual reader.

Column No 216: June 14, 2009

Reading the Almanac (What to do Today?)

English translations of the calendar section of the Chinese Almanac list the Gregorian date and its element-animal combination; for instance, June 21, 2009 was the Day of the Fire Rooster. Identifying the combination of the day is vital for a feng shui master to be able to calculate whether it is suitable for various activities pertaining to an individual, a family or their property.

As it happens, that day was not a particularly good day to do anything, at home or out. Marking the end of the 15-day lunar cycle, it is denoted as a *chi* or shifting energy day, which means it is generally considered to be inauspicious for activities such as weddings, signing contracts and moving house. July 5 in the same year, by contrast, will be a good day to move into a new property, position your bed and stove, install an altar and raise a roofing beam.

The almanac lists appropriate days for activities ranging from cremation and burial to washing and cutting one's hair.

In our modern age, it would be cumbersome if one were to limit one's visit to the hairdresser to a few days a month. However, when it comes to life-changing activities such as moving home or getting married, it is recommended you select an appropriately auspicious date.

Column No 217: June 21, 2009

Reading the Almanac 2 (Time To Act)

The calendar section of the Chinese Almanac does not only identify recommended and inauspicious activities for a specific date, it also does the same for hours of the day. According to Chinese metaphysics, the day is divided into 12 units of two hours each, with each unit corresponding to one of the animals of the Chinese zodiac.

Thus the time of the Ox runs from 1am to 3am and the time of the Horse starts at 11am. Feng Shui masters will suggest doing certain activities at certain times of the day but, of course, it may not be feasible to time wedding ceremonies for the wee hours of the morning.

The almanac also lists the governing energy, represented by the Flying Star of a day, to enable feng shui masters to calculate which sectors are positive or negative. The negative direction of the day, i.e. the *San Shar* or Three Killings direction, is also identified, and it would be inadvisable to carry out drilling, digging or construction in certain sectors (the cardinal directions, north, west, south and east).

The element-animal combination that clashes with each day is also identified: for example July 12, 2009 is the day of the Earth Horse, which clashes with, and is thus inauspicious for, those born in the Water Rat year of 1972.

Column No 218: June 28, 2009

Date Selection Formulas (Timing Is Everything)

There are auspicious and inauspicious times at which to undertake certain tasks, or celebrate. Two of the main means of date selection, as determined by Chinese astrology, are the 12 Day Officers and the 28 Lunar Constellations methods. The former has the days repeating in a sequence of 12, while the latter has the days repeating in a cycle of 28.

Feng Shui masters will thus identify the most appropriate day for a particular purpose using one or both of these methods.

While the specifics of these two methods are complicated, the most important factor with regard to date selection is a person's year of birth, and not the month, day or hour of birth. This is represented by your Chinese zodiac animal. For those born in January or the first half of February, note that what determines your animal is not the lunar New Year date but the solar New Year, which usually falls on February 4/5th.

The worst date on which to plan something for any individual is one that clashes with their zodiac animal. For instance, according to the 12 Day Officers method, those born in the Year of the Ox (1997, 1985, 1973, etc) should avoid planning anything for a Sheep day, while the Dog day is not recommended for those born in the Year of the Dragon (2000, 1988, 1976 etc). Other clashes include Rat-Horse, Tiger-Monkey, Rabbit-Rooster and Snake-Pig.

Column No 219: July 5, 2009

Date Selection for Weddings (Union Rules)

You may have noticed that on certain days in Hong Kong, marriage registries are busy places and hotel conference rooms are fully booked out with wedding banquets and celebrations. Conversely, during the Festival of Hungry Ghosts (the seventh month of the lunar calendar, which roughly corresponds to the month of August), there aren't too many couples getting hitched, and hotels offer significant discounts to those wishing to hire their conference rooms. This can be attributed to the belief that certain periods or days are auspicious (or not) for specific activities.

The Chinese almanac of dates, or the *Tong Shu*, lists days that are suitable for weddings but these are considered auspicious from a general point of view only.

Feng Shui masters will take into account the time and date of birth of the groom and bride to select the most auspicious date to celebrate their union. Dates that clash with the couple's year or day of birth will be avoided, as will those that conflict with the year or month that celebrations will be held (note: celebrations may not take place on the day of the wedding.)

The time at which wedding celebrations begin will be specified within a two-hour period, as per the practice of measuring time in units of two hours, ruled one of the 12 zodiac animals.

Column No 226: August 23, 2009

Date Selection for Moving (On the Move)

It is important when relocating to a new home or office to do so at an auspicious time, to maximize the benefits of the move. Feng Shui masters state that timing is another facet of Chinese metaphysics and moving home at an inauspicious time may negate otherwise favourable aspects of a place.

While the Chinese almanac, or *Tong Shu*, may list certain dates and times as being auspicious, note that these are not tailored to an individual. A feng shui master would have to factor in the astrological data of all family members and ensure that the moving date does not clash with the year of birth of any of them, especially that of the head of the household.

An additional element is the orientation of a property. Each of the 12 Chinese zodiac animals are associated with a specific direction; it is important to ensure that the day on which the move occurs does not clash with the orientation – and animal – of a home or office. If your home faces north (represented by the Rat), you should not move on the day of the Horse (which clashes with the Rat).

A feng shui master will also specify the time at which the move should start. He will pick a two-hour period in which this should happen, although the time the move is actually completed is not as important.

Column No 227: August 30, 2009

Date Selection for Babies (Bringing Up Baby)

With the trend of expectant mothers booking a Caesarian section months in advance, feng shui masters are increasingly being consulted as to when new additions to the family should be delivered. This involves consulting astrological birth charts for various dates then identifying the one that is most appropriate. This will determine a child's destiny, so must be carried out by an experienced consultant.

From a feng shui perspective, the main consideration is that the child's chart should not clash with those of its parents. Timings that will produce an individual with as few health problems as possible are given preference over those that would provide opportunities for wealth and success. The master will also try to minimise the period of time in which an individual will have bad luck.

Masters are constrained by practical considerations, of course – it is doubtful parents will be able to a book a birth in the early hours of a Sunday morning, for example – and there may be unforeseen circumstances such as power outages and traffic jams that may scupper the best-laid plans.

But such things fall within the heaven-luck-component of a person's life; if a child isn't 'meant' to be born at a certain time, it won't happen.

Column No 228: September 6, 2009

The 24 Solar Terms (Sun Days)

You may have noticed that Chinese solar months start at some point between the fourth and eighth day of a Western month.

For instance, the ninth solar month of the Chinese calendar (the Month of the Dog) starts on October 8 and runs until November 6 in 2009. This is dictated by the use of the 24 solar terms or *jie chi* in feng shui calculations. The 12 *jie* mark the beginning of a month and the 12 *chi* mark their midpoints.

Solar terms are used to indicate climatic and agricultural conditions, important to agrarian communities in days gone by. The first solar term, the beginning of spring or Li Chun, which mostly falls on February 4th, marks the beginning of the solar year. The festival of *Ching Ming* is identified by the fifth solar term and usually falls on April 5th.

The midpoints of the months coincide with Western benchmarks - the spring equinox or *Chiu Fen* (fourth solar term) was on March 20 in 2009, and the winter solstice or Dong Zhi (the end of winter) will be on December 22.

The 24 solar markers are used by feng shui masters to help schedule festivals and occasions such as burials. They are also marked on *luo pans* (feng shui compasses).

Column 233: October 11, 2009

Date Selection Clashes (Clash Course)

As already mentioned, when it comes to selecting your wedding date, avoiding the animal that clashes with your year of birth is crucial. The six pairings that clash are the rat with the horse, ox/sheep, tiger/monkey, rabbit/rooster, dragon/dog and snake/pig. Therefore, a couple born in the years of the rooster and dog should avoid getting married on either a rabbit or dragon day. The animals that characterize each day are stated in the Chinese almanac, or *Tong Shu*, which is available before the start of each year, in Chinese and English.

These types of clashes are also to be avoided when planning certain other activities. For instance, in the Year of the Tiger, feng shui masters would advise against opening a business or signing a contract in a monkey month or on a monkey day, as they clash with the year. As each month correlates to one animal, the days that clash with a month's animal should also be avoided.

For example, in the Month of the Ox, the sheep days (January 14 and 26) are not recommended for important activities. In February, the Month of the Tiger, the monkey days (February 15 and 27) are the ones to avoid.

When there is no alternative but to hold an event during a month that clashes, feng shui masters will choose a day on which other factors combine to alleviate the effects of the clash.

Column No 244: January 3, 2010

Date Selection for Moving (In the Right Direction)

When it comes to selecting a date to move into a property, not only is the year of birth of the main occupants taken into account, but so is the direction in which the property lies. For instance, if your property faces north, it is represented by the horse and you should not move on a day of the rat, as that creature clashes with the sitting direction of your property.

Some feng shui masters will also advise against an individual sleeping with his head pointing towards, or working at a desk with their back against, the direction that clashes with their year of birth. Having a property facing your 'clashing' direction is not an issue, however.

Although personal clashes are used in calculations involving date selection it is important to note that there are several other factors to consider. A couple born in the years of the snake and pig, for instance, are not necessarily destined for divorce.

Animals and elements representing the days, months and hours of birth should be analysed before the compatibility of a couple is determined and, when it comes to interpersonal relationships, a skilled astrologer will identify all troublesome elements and take a nuanced view of how they impact with a partner's chart.

Column No 245: January 10, 2010

Chapter 6

Festivals

Lunar New Year Preparations (Fresh Start)

To usher in the Lunar New Year, spring cleaning is needed to remove the dirt and negative energy that has accumulated in the home in the previous 12 months. Traditionally, furniture is rearranged and cleaned, as are windows, walls and ceilings. Kitchen utensils and bed line are also washed. It is vital that spring cleaning is completed by Lunar New Year's Eve, otherwise you enter the New Year with tasks outstanding.

On New Year's Eve, families gather, either at home or at their favourite restaurant, for the final meal of the old year. Traditionally, children are allowed to stay up until midnight to greet the New Year. Another common practice is to place red scrolls with rhyming couplets on the front door or in the living room. These scrolls contain four characters and are basically blessings for the New Year and pleas for things such as good health, the accomplishment of 10,000 tasks and the achievement of goals.

The Chinese character for fortune (*fuk*) is also prominently displayed upside-down because 'upside-down' is pronounced the same way as 'arrive' in spoken Chinese. Thus, 'fortune' written upside-down symbolises fortune arriving.

It is also vital to settle any debt and loans so you can start the New Year with a clean slate.

Column No 45: January 15, 2006

Lunar New Year Taboos (Avoidance Therapy)

Traditionally, Chinese think that whatever happens on Lunar New Year's Day will reflect one's fortunes for the rest of the year. Therefore, there are certain practices that should be avoided on this day to ensure the rest of the year goes smoothly.

Avoid using a broom, as it is believed this may sweep away one's good fortune and new opportunities. If sweeping has to be done, start from the sides of the room and sweep towards the centre. The accumulated rubbish should be left in a corner and thrown away the next day.

Knives and scissors should also not be used on this day. Traditionally, a piece of red string (representing fire) is tied around the metal portions of these utensils, so as to control the negative metal energy. Use of these cutting instruments on the first day implies interpersonal conflicts and the deterioration and subsequent severance of relationships and ties.

One should also not demand repayment of loans on the first day of a New Year, while arguing and fighting on this day will imply stress and conflict for the rest of the year.

Another popular belief is that washing one's hair on this day will wash away the year's good luck.

Column No 46: January 22, 2006

Beating the Small Individuals (Just Beat It)

In the Chinese almanac, March 6 (plus or minus a few days) is the Day of Waking Insects, which represents spring getting into full swing. On this day, it is traditionally believed all creatures awaken from their hibernation and start gathering food for the following winter. In olden days, this included the tiger, which would prey on humans. Thus, this also marks the day when offerings are made to the white tiger spirit.

As tiger numbers diminished, the day became one in which people dealt with the 'small people' (*siu yun*) in their lives. Small individuals are those with malicious intentions who hinder you or gossip behind your back. 'Beating' them ensures their negativity will not affect the rest of your year.

Write the name of your enemy on a piece of paper and then use a wooden clog or slipper to beat it while chanting what you would like to do to them. Carry out this ritual in a quiet spot because doing it in a busy area will increase the possibility of your enemy slipping out of your grasp. Pictures of animals can also be used to symbolise the qualities of your adversaries, for example a pig represents laziness, a snake spitefulness and a tiger aggression.

Some feng shui masters believe this ritual just allows us to therapeutically release our frustration and dissatisfaction against the unfair events in our lives.

Column No 51: March 5, 2006

All Souls' Day (Soul Survivors)

Ching Ming is the Chinese version of All Souls' Day. *Ching* means 'clear' while *ming* implies 'bright'. Thus, during a clear and bright time – spring - the deceased are honoured and remembered. Filial duties to one's ancestors are carried out in the form of cleaning and sweeping their graves.

The conception of ancestral 'worship' is derived from the belief the spirit survives after death and is aware of the behaviour and conduct of those left behind. It is thought that if one's ancestors are respected and tended to by their descendants, they can extend their assistance and positive influence to their descendants.

Therefore, families go to their ancestors' cemeteries to pay their respects, tidy the graves, plant new bushes and trees and repaint the inscriptions on the tombstones or tablets. Offerings are also made, such as food, drinks, flowers and paper money, which is meant for use in the world beyond. Made from joss paper, they are burned at the graves.

It is vital to pray to the deceased with sincerity. Ancestors will not bestow their blessings on those who perform prayers casually and unwillingly. It is also thought to be unwise to take photographs at a cemetery or temple because this may offend the deceased.

Column No 55: April 2, 2006

'Evil Month' (Resident Evil)

In ancient China, the fifth lunar month, referred to as Lunar May by some feng shui masters, was considered the 'evil month' because its hot and humid weather suits insects, parasites and bacteria; it is a month of infestations and pestilence.

Not to be confused with the Hungry Ghosts' Festival of the seventh lunar month, the 'evil month' was believed to be ruled by the five gods of plagues. Several techniques were employed to curb these malicious gods. These included burning realgar, a reddish mineral that produces yellow smoke and an offensive odour that is thought to exterminate insects. Cakes in the shape of the five poisonous creatures (scorpion, centipede, lizard, snake and spider) were sold and consumed, in the belief symbolic poison served as an antidote to actual venom.

Images of demon slayer Zhong Kui and yellow paper inscribed with scriptures were also posted inside and outside the houses as protection.

The fifth month is considered to be an inauspicious time to carry out important activities such as moving house, getting married or starting a new enterprise. Yet, the month needn't be a total washout; experienced feng shui masters will tailor the timing of important events to an individual's birth data and the orientation and layout of their property.

Column No 62: May 21, 2006

Hungry Ghosts' Festival (Soothing the Spirits)

Yue Lan, the Hungry Ghosts Festival, falls on the 14th day of the seventh lunar month. During this month-long period, it is believed the gates of the underworld are open, allowing spirits to wander the world of the living. Offerings and prayers are made to placate and comfort these hungry ghosts.

These unhappy spirits are those who have died without descendants, or those who experienced violent deaths and were not given proper funeral rites. If not placated, the spirits may disturb the living. Offerings of incense, paper clothing, food and spirit money are made at roadsides, temples, intersections and other open spaces, while makeshift tents housing altars are also erected against settings of giant joss-sticks. The placated spirits are then supposed to return to the underworld before the arrival of the 8th moon.

Feng Shui masters advise clients not to get married, move or start new businesses during this period. You may also find banquet venues offering heavily discounted rates for the duration of the festival.

When passing spirit offerings on the street, it is insensitive and inadvisable to step over them, to spit or to show other signs of disrespect. The older generation may also be reluctant to go out during this month.

Column No 73: August 6, 2006

Double Nine Festival (Double Celebration)

The *Chung Yang*, or Double-Nine, Festival occurs on the ninth day of the ninth lunar month. In the *I Ching* (the Chinese Book of Changes), nine is considered a yang number, which explains why on the 'double-nine' day there is significant yang energy.

In Hong Kong, the *Chung Yang* Festival is one of two annual occasions on which one's ancestors are commemorated, the other being *Ching Ming*. Food offerings (rice, vegetarian food, fruit, tea and wine) are placed for the ancestors in front of their tombs and shrines. Spirit money is also burnt, then scattered in all directions.

With the clear autumn skies and pleasant weather, there has also been a tradition of climbing mountains on the double-nine day. The belief is that by ascending to these heights one will be able to avoid misfortune, attain a higher position and lead a long, healthy life.

This originated from a Han-dynasty legend in which a man was advised by a hermit to climb a mountain on this day to avoid a catastrophe. He paid no heed to the warning and returned home with his family to discover his poultry and cattle dead. Chrysanthemums, the flower of longevity, are worn or attached to windows and doors during this period to ensure good fortune.

Column No 86: November 5. 2006

Winter Solstice (Long and Short of It)

The winter solstice falls on December 22 in the Chinese calendar. In the northern hemisphere, it is the shortest day of the year, with daylight (yang energy) at its minimum and night (yin energy) at its maximum. Hence, it is considered the coldest day of the year. More importantly, it marks the transition between winter and spring, because it indicates warm weather is soon to arrive.

In ancient China, the festival was a major event, as it meant farmers could start spring cultivation. In the Imperial era, the emperor would lead the annual sacrifices at the Temple of Heaven in Beijing, a procession that foreigners and most Chinese were forbidden to witness. In modern Hong Kong, a significant number of companies still give their employees the afternoon off for the occasion.

Most Hong Kong families mark this night by reuniting for a feast, which will include glutinous rice dumplings served towards the end of the meal. Offerings are made to ancestors and family members who travel a lot, and return home as a sign of respect to their forebears, and to show they have reached their destination for the year. The winter solstice is also seen as a time when everyone is essentially a year older, even though the year is not officially over.

Column No 91: December 10, 2006

Solar New Year (Solar Power)

While the Lunar New Year, which marks the start of Chinese New Year, falls at various dates in January and February, astrologers and feng shui masters use the Solar New Year for calculations and to demarcate the New Year. It generally falls on 4th/5th February.

Most Chinese festivals are marked by the traditional lunar calendar, which measures the rotation of the moon around the Earth. There are approximately 29.5 days between one moon and the next, which means 12 revolutions will take 354 days. The solar calendar measures the rotation around the sun of the Earth, which takes 365.25 days to make a full revolution. To account for the 11-day difference between the two calendars, a lunar leap month of about 30 days is added every two or three years. To be precise, each 19-year period will have seven years in which an additional month is added.

As the lunar calendar marks the appearance of the full moon, in the days before the invention of the electric light it was a social occasion.

The more uniform solar calendar became the basis for agricultural calculations and Chinese metaphysics such as astrology and feng shui. Classically trained feng shui masters will tell you, therefore, that those born before February 4th/5th belong to the previous Chinese Solar Year.

Column No 98: February 4, 2007

Pre Lunar New Year Rituals (In With the New)

Rituals to usher in the lunar New Year usually start on the 24th day of the 12th lunar month. To mark the *Tse Tso* (thanking the stove) ceremony, there is a thorough cleaning of homes. Homage is paid to the kitchen god (*Tso Kwan*) because it is believed he appears before the Jade Emperor in heaven to report on the behaviour of the members of the household.

To gain favour, Tso Kwan's shrine is cleaned thoroughly and he is given a delicious meal of glutinous rice and honey, which may be smeared on his mouth to ensure what he says will be flattering and sweet. A generous amount of spirit money is burned to assist him with his travel expenses.

Vertical red banners covered with auspicious phrases written in black or gold ink are placed on the main door and across the entrance. They usually refer to health, wealth and longevity and exhort positive outcomes.

Pictures of the door gods, two generals in full military armour, are placed on the front gates to protect against evil spirits.

An ancient Taoist legend states the door gods were two brothers who lived under an enormous peach tree and protected mankind by catching demons and throwing them to tigers. Others believe that they are two loyal soldiers who guarded a Tang-dynasty emperor while he was asleep.

Column No 99: February 11, 2007

The Lantern Festival (Good Moon Rising)

The *Yuen Siu*, or Lantern Festival, is held on the 15th day of the 1st lunar month. It celebrates the first full moon of the year and originated as a ceremony that ushered in the warmth and light of the season following the winter cold. The lantern aspect probably stems from a Tang-dynasty emperor who built 30 lantern towers to celebrate the full moon.

In ancient China, families lit up as many lanterns as there were family members. Extra ones would be hung for those hoping to have babies in the New Year. Lanterns also served as signposts for the spirits of ancestors, guiding them to the celebrations and back to the world beyond. Traditionally, riddles regarding Chinese language, geography and history were written on slips of paper pasted on the lanterns. People who solved them would be rewarded on the spot.

The Lantern Festival was also a time when young women were able to walk around town unchaperoned, allowing professional matchmakers to seek partners for them. Women wanting a husband would cast oranges into the sea while uttering couplets; young men would throw apples wishing for a good wife. Longans would be thrown for the good things in life, pebbles for a house and coins for prosperity and wealth in the New Year.

Column No 101: March 4, 2007

Graves (Grave Dangers)

The *Ching Ming* Festival is when Chinese families visit cemeteries or columbariums to pay respect to their ancestors. Graves are swept by the descendants of the deceased, prayers are said and food offerings made. Some feng shui principles govern the design and location of graves, also known as 'yin houses.'

The Chinese believe the position or feng shui of a grave will affect the lives of future generations. Yin-house feng shui developed from a time when people were free to bury family members in any undeveloped area. To assess the feng shui of a burial ground, the nature and shape of surrounding mountains is taken into account.

Ideally, there should be water present in the vicinity, with emphasis placed on the way the water flows, its clarity and volume. Clear water that pools in a lake in front of a site before meandering out is preferable to polluted water that flows straight past. It is also important to select an appropriate date for carrying out the last rites, and an internment.

Even though modern dense urban living dictates that only specific areas are suitable for burial, appropriate sites can still be recommended by experienced yin-house feng shui masters.

Column No 106: April 8, 2007

Mid Autumn Festival (Cry for the Moon)

According to the Chinese lunar calendar, autumn occurs during the seventh, eighth and ninth lunar months. Hence, the 15th day of the eighth month marks the Mid-Autumn Festival. Also known as the Mooncake or Lantern Festival, the mid-autumn day was used to celebrate the season's harvest in ancient China.

In traditional China, the Mid-Autumn festival was a woman's occasion, being associated with the moon, a yin symbol. Each family had a an outdoor table that faced the moon and on which they placed round fruit (reflecting the moon's shape) such as apples, oranges, peaches and pomegranates as well as mooncakes and cups of wine and tea. Single women would pray to meet a life partner while those who were married would wish for healthy, intelligent offspring. Legend had it men should not participate in the rituals for this festival, as they might absorb the great yin energy of the moon, causing them to become effeminate.

Elders usually warn children against pointing at the moon, as it is considered disrespectful and the moon might 'slice' their ear as punishment. It is something to note if you want to avoid waking up with a scabby line behind your ear.

Column No 130: September 23, 2007

Red Packets (In the Red)

Known as *hong bao* in Putonghua and *lai see* in Cantonese, red packets containing 'lucky money' are presented to children and single adults during Lunar New Year celebrations.

The money enclosed in these red envelopes should be of an even amount (for example: $80, $100 or $200), which is considered auspicious. It should not be an amount starting or ending with the number four, which represents 'death' in both languages. Each adult usually gives one packet, which is why married couples will give two. Unmarried individuals are not expected to hand out lucky money.

The word *hong* implies 'vast', thereby suggesting the money will multiply. It's believed that giving and receiving red packets brings good fortune to all, as those who give will, in turn, receive. Those who receive should thank the giver graciously, saying *do jeh* in Cantonese or *xie xie* in Putonghua. The envelopes should not be opened in the presence of the giver, otherwise bad luck will befall the receiver. Lucky money should be saved.

In Asia, feng shui consultants receive *lai see* from their clients. The clients use their judgment to give an amount commensurate with the expertise of the master. Failing to do so will bring bad luck.

Column No 147: January 27, 2008

Firecrackers (Say it Loud)

The thunder of firecrackers marks the advent of the Lunar New Year. It is believed the noise scares away evil spirits and repels negative energy, bringing forth auspicious energy for the New Year.

According to legend, Chinese villagers were stalked by the man-eating monster Nian at the end of every lunar year. When the powerful star god Tzu Wei discovered the beast was afraid of the colour red and loud noises, villagers were advised to adorn themselves and their homes in that hue and create as much of a racket as possible.

Hence, on Lunar New Year's Eve, red lanterns and red strips of paper with lettering were hung on each home and everyone wore scarlet as they played drums and gongs and exploded fire crackers. The terrified Nian fled into the mountains and, from that day onwards, successive generations carried out Tzu's recommendations so the beast would never return.

Nowadays, these traditions are observed to dispel the misfortune and tribulations of the previous year and beckon good health, happiness and prosperity for the year ahead. Firecrackers can be lit at home, shops and offices. The lucky red confetti and remnants of firecrackers are removed a few days after the celebrations.

Column No 148: February 3, 2008

Seasonal Flowers and Plants (Petal Power)

The Lunar New Year holiday season is one of the few occasions in Chinese culture, other than at funerals, or business openings, when the giving of flowers is common. While red flowers are considered auspicious, one should never give white flowers as that is the colour of mourning. Kumquat plants are popular at this time because they represent gold and prosperity. Peach flowers symbolise long life while the peony indicates wealth. The plum blossom implies friendship and perseverance, and the evergreen cypress and pine, vitality and endurance.

Prosperity trees, such as miniature citrus plants, will have had old coins and red envelopes tied to their branches with red string as an offering to the god of wealth. Oranges, tangerines and mandarins will have been offered in pairs to elders by the younger generation to symbolise prosperity and good health in the coming year.

In traditional feng shui, plants and flowers represent the wood element, which has both positive (academic study and romance) and negative (stress and overwork) associations. To increase the potential in your personal and professional life this year, place plants or flowers in the northeast or southeast sectors of your home. If your bathroom or kitchen are in these sectors, consult a feng shui professional.

Column No 149: February 17, 2008

Lunar New Year (New Eras)

The Lunar New Year is also known in Putonghua as *Yuan Dan*, which means beginning and morning. Thus, the new moon in the first lunar month of the year heralds a new cycle, starting at dawn. It is known as *Chun Jie* or the Spring Festival and brings renewed hope for a bountiful spring, especially after a long or harsh winter.

The Spring Festival is marked by the lunar calendar, which measures the period between each full moon, usually 29 or 30 days. An additional lunar month is added every two to three years as a kind of 'leap month', which brings it back in line with the Gregorian or solar calendar.

The solar calendar, which measures the length of time the Earth takes to travel around the sun, has a total of 365.25 days.

The difference between the lunar and solar calendars explains why the Spring Festival might fall on February 7 one year, and on February 14 the next.

Most feng shui masters do not use the Spring Festival's date to identify a person's zodiac sign. Rather, the beginning of Spring, denoted on the solar calendar as February 4th or 5th, is observed as the transition point.

Column No 197: February 1, 2009

Chapter 7

Decorations and Symbols

Guardian Lions (On Guard)

Standing guard outside many office buildings, hotels and homes in Asia are pairs of imposing stone lions. Also known as Fu dogs, they are thought to protect against negative energy.

To differentiate between the male and female lions, look at the object underneath their paws. The male lion rests his paw on a ball or pearl, while the female rests her paw on a curled-up cub. Standing with your back to your front door, the male lion should be on your left and the female on your right. Should they be placed the other way round, women will be in control in that household.

A famous hotel in Taipei, which has the female lion on the left and the male on the right, has always had female managing directors. When a male director took over, complications arose, the worst of which was a fire that seriously damaged the hotel. Order was restored when a female director was appointed.

Miniature stone lions are widely available in shops in Hong Kong and can be seen sitting at the entrance of apartments that face the emergency stairs or a lift. Traditionally, it's believed the lions will be effective only if they have gone through an official blessing ceremony carried out by Taoist monks, usually performed at the inauguration of new buildings.

Column No 25: August 21, 2005

Plants (Back to Nature)

In densely populated cities such as Hong Kong, it is still possible to find room for plants in the home, either in the lounge or dining-room. According to feng shui, it is not advisable to place plants in a bedroom as they compete with the occupants for oxygen. If you have plants in your bedroom, it is likely you will wake up feeling lethargic, even after considerable periods of rest.

It is also not advisable to have plants with thorns, such as cacti, or creepers that may overwhelm the walls (even on your balcony), as this could result in increased conflict and unwanted gossip.

While small pine or Christmas trees may be welcome seasonal additions to the house, having them indoors year-round may result in a loss of wealth due to their needle-shaped leaves. Peach blossom trees can add a touch of romance to your life but excessive numbers or extremely large plants could cause romantic complications and entanglements.

The general rule is you choose green plants with leaves that are not too sharp and will not spread too far. Balconies overrun by plants become focal points for yin energy, and too much of this can adversely affect the health of the occupants of a home. Keep plants healthy and make sure they are placed in the proper sectors of your home, this will ensure you enjoy good health and wealth.

Column No 28: September 11, 2005

Clocks (Time on Your Side)

Clocks denote the passing of time, which is why there are certain guidelines to follow with regard to their placement in the home. For instance, clocks should not be positioned directly opposite or above the main entrance, as this implies that occupants will be placed under pressure in their daily lives. It is also not advisable to locate a clock directly opposite portraits or photos of family members, as this suggests their time is running out. Having too many clocks displayed prominently will increase anxiety, as one is constantly reminded of time passing either slowly or quickly, depending on one's life circumstances.

Moreover, clocks should never be given as presents. In Cantonese, the word for clock rhymes with the word for the end. Thereby, giving someone a clock equates to paying one's final respects. Should you find yourself in this awkward situation, you can alleviate the problem by giving the recipient a token sum of money, for example $1, so it appears you are paying for the clock.

Clocks also serve a purpose in classical feng shui. Positioned appropriately, their metallic quality and constant activity can reduce negative, or stimulate positive, metal energies. Positioned inappropriately, they will aggravate occupants, making them impatient and quick-tempered.

Column No 58: April 23, 2006

Coins (Sides of the Coin)

Browsing through the Sunday markets in Hong Kong, and in Chinatowns in other cities, you may have come across traditional Chinese coins. Circular but with a square hole in the centre, these gold coins have Chinese symbols on one side and characters on the other. The characters state the name of the Qing emperor from whose reign the coins date. Nowadays, feng shui masters employ the coins as cures and enhancers, with their metallic nature used to alleviate areas afflicted with negative earth energy.

Coins are placed in groups of five or six then laid in a straight line. They should be placed discreetly; under floor mats or above doors. Sometimes, they are buried under the floor during construction. In offices, placing coins under desks will be more effective than putting them on phones and computer screens because drawing attention to feng shui cures may attract unwanted negative attention.

Some feng shui masters advocate using coins only from the reign of the emperors from the first half of the Qing dynasty, when it was at its peak: Emperors Shunzhi, Kangxi, Yongzheng, Qianlong and Jiaqing. Supposedly, should you use coins from later emperors, the results may be less than ideal. Three coins can also be tied with a red string and placed in one's wallet to imply a constant flow of wealth.

Column No 60: May 7, 2006

Wind Chimes (Something in the Air)

For some western readers, wind chimes have come to represent feng shui. Modern feng shui consultants advocate their placement within a residence, saying the soothing sounds they make have a calming influence. However, some classical feng shui masters disagree.

Traditionally, the sound of a wind chime is used to dispel negative energy present in a specific location. It is vital is the rods are made of metal, as should the central piece that knocks against them to create the sound. Glass rods and wooden centrepieces are not recommended, as they do not conform to traditional design. Some masters feel five-or six-rod chimes are preferable as they conform to certain feng shui calculations. Whether the rods are solid or hollow is not important.

Obviously, wind chimes should be hung where there are air currents, as silent chimes have no beneficial effects. But if you hang wind chimes on your balcony, be aware the sound produced on windy days may be unsettling for you - and your neighbours.

There is also a school of thought that believes wind chimes have the ability to attract spirits, which is why it is advisable to consult a professional feng shui consultant as opposed to hanging up your wind chime indiscriminately.

Column No 61: May 14, 2006

Photos (Photo Finish)

There are certain guidelines to adhere to when displaying photos in your home. Photographs of family members and friends should not be hung at a level below the waist, as this is considered disrespectful. For instance, if photos were at feet level, then one would be inadvertently kicking or walking on the images of loved ones. Also, photos should not be placed directly opposite toilet doors or at the end of long corridors.

Although pictures of deceased family members can be placed with other photos, it is not advisable to display excessively large portraits, which may overwhelm a room. This is due to the fact that residences are yang domains and images of the dearly departed are yin in nature.

Similarly, having photos of older family members in the bedroom is not recommended, as the bedroom is an area for private activity. It is also prudent to review your displayed photos regularly. If there are numerous pictures of you with a former partner or friends that you have lost contact with, this may preclude new social opportunities in your life. For couples, it is better to have photos of you together rather than many of one of the other, as that does not augur well for your relationship.

Finally, if a photo frame is chipped or the glass surface cracked, replace it immediately.

Column 63: May 28, 2006

Animal Pictures (Wild Things)

You may have seen images of running horses (usually in groups of eight) on the walls of Chinese business premises. Chances are you didn't realise the prints are placed so the horses run into, rather than out of, the office or restaurant. This is because horses signify professional success; having them 'run' out of the door would be akin to opportunities slipping from a person's grasp. Ensure the prints are hung so their bodies 'move' inwards and away from the main door.

While images of aggressive animals such as tigers, lions and bears in the boardroom may convey professional power, placing them in the home is inappropriate. Images of these animals in the bedroom may result in insomnia and restlessness for the occupants, while their presence in the living and dining rooms may cause family arguments.

Placing them opposite or adjacent to family photographs may lead to health problems. The only appropriate place for pictures of these powerful animals is outside the living space, next to the front door, to deter unwanted visitors.

Some feng shui masters may suggest clients place images of Chinese cultural symbols, such as the dragon and phoenix, for health and wealth in their homes, but the cultural sensitivities and personal taste of the occupants should also be taken into account.

Column No 64: June 4, 2006

Water Pictures (Water, Water Everywhere)

Placing images of water in your home does not necessarily lead to immediate wealth, because there are several factors to take into account. For instance, if the picture is of a river, its course should flow into the house from the direction of the front door. If it flows towards the front door, finances could be drained.

It's best to have pictures of calm water, such as lakes, rivers and bays, in the home. Images of ships struggling in turbulent seas might lead to obstacles and difficulties in the occupants' lives. Scenes in the study featuring stormy water may result in professional or academic setbacks, while having them in the bedroom may lead to unexpected traumas. Waterfalls represent passion and situations that are unstable; it is not advisable to place such images in living areas unless you want to attract excitement and thrills.

In the bedroom, images of water - still or turbulent – might be overwhelming, especially if placed above the occupants' heads.

In classical feng shui, water not only represents wealth, but also intelligence and romance. Having inappropriate prints of water in your master bedroom will see an increased possibility of unwanted romantic entanglements and complications.

Column No 65: June 11, 2006

Romance Pictures (Pictures of Romance)

If you are on the hunt for a romantic partner, it's not a good idea to hang pictures of solitary men or women in your living area, especially those of unhappy figures.

Single men should avoid images of male-oriented pursuits and sportsmen, while single women should steer clear of displaying too many images of female friends and role models, and ex-partners.

Feng shui principles don't call for you to display images that go against your interests; it would be unreasonable to expect men to display pictures of women embroidering (unless they are into that sort of thing, of course). Rather, balance is advocated; instead of only having images of role models of the same sex, there should also be those of the opposite gender. Images of happy couples will also augur well for one's romantic prospects.

While memories of previous joyous relationships should be cherished, having mementoes take pride of place in the home won't leave any room for new romantic opportunities.

The elements associated with romance are wood and water. Classically trained feng shui masters can identify the romance corner of the home, where images of wood and water, or plants and water features, should be placed to boost one's romantic prospects.

Column No 66: June 18, 2006

Abstract Versus Nature (Abstract Ideas)

Feng Shui masters tend to be uncomfortable with abstract art hung on the walls of homes as such pieces can be extremely yin or yang in nature. For instance, while bright splashes of colour on a red background will be more suited to a living room than a bedroom due to their yang nature, they may cause the room's occupants to become agitated and unsettled.

A predominantly dark piece with silhouettes of the human form may appear too foreboding and threatening for children. Some pieces of abstract art lack balance and form and are better suited to commercial premises than residences. Each piece should be assessed individually.

In contrast, images of natural scenery like mountains are popular as they denote stability. Having an image of a verdant, gently undulating mountain (as opposed to a sharp, jagged peak or a volcano) behind one's chair in the study confers support for one's endeavours. If there is water in the form of a lake or river at the base of the mountain, ensure it does not overwhelm the mountain in the image, as having water behind one's back signifies instability and unpredictability.

Some feng shui masters feel that if their client's unfavourable element is earth (as calculated using their astrology chart), placing a picture of a mountain behind them is not to be recommended.

Column No 67: June 25, 2006

117

Wu Lou Gourd (Turn to the Bottle)

You may have noticed the bottle gourd or calabash in Chinese medicine shops. Known in Cantonese as the *wu lou* and in Mandarin as the *hu lu*, it is shaped like a figure of eight with a lip protrusion at the top. This gourd is believed to embody Heaven and Earth, and contain energy that wards off evil spirits. It is used in traditional feng shui to absorb negative energy associated with illness and can be worn or placed within the home. It does not need to be prominently displayed and can be unobtrusively put adjacent to or under the bed, or in a cabinet in a hallway; its positioning depends on the location of the sickness energy.

The connection between the gourd and good health probably derived from its shape, which made it ideal as a receptacle for medicine. In Chinese art, calabashes are often see on the backs of elderly men, further cementing their status as symbols of longevity.

For practical feng shui purposes, you can use a natural, dried calabash or ones made of metal such as silver or copper.

Alternatively, the gourd design can be incorporated into a living space through soft-furnishing designs or prints. Some feng shui masters recommend hanging jade calabashes around wrists or in vehicles for protection.

Column No 74: August 13, 2006

Paintings and Stones (Set In Stone)

At the entrance to some traditional buildings situated at T-junctions or sandwiched between two roads, stone tablets bearing Chinese characters may be observed. While they might look like tombstones, they are actually a classical feng shui protective device, known as the *shih kan tang* or resisting stones.

Resisting stones block the sharp attacking energy that is generated from a straight road or bridge pointing towards a building. When a building is located in between two converging roads (as in the case of a Y or scissors junction), the stone prevents the building from being overwhelmed or cut by the surrounding roads. Resisting stones may be decorated with an image of the head of a lion with a sword held in its teeth, the yin yang symbol or eight trigrams. They are considered miniature versions of one of the eight sacred Taoist mountains of China, such as Mount Tai Shan. Indeed, the Chinese characters on these stones usually read Tai Shan Mountain Resisting Stone.

You may have also observed paintings of mountains and water placed at the entrance to homes situated at intersections. Known as *shan hai zhen* or mountain sea stability images, it is believed that the water and earth present in these depictions will nullify the fire energy that is approaching from incoming roads.

Column No 162: May 18, 2008

Lucky Cats (Paws for Thought)

You may have noticed porcelain cats with one raised paw located at the cash register of local shops and restaurants. These cats are considered symbols of good fortune and called *choy mao* ('wealth cat') in Cantonese. They originated in Japan, where they are known as *maneki neko* ('beckoning cat'), and some examples, dating back to the 18th century, are displayed in museums. However, their precise origins are unknown.

If the left paw of the cat is raised, it is believed to beckon guests or customers. When the right paw is lifted, the cat is said to bring financial prosperity. Thus, business owners may prefer to have a cat with its right paw raised, while restaurants will opt for a statue with its left paw beckoning. Alternatively, you may display a pair of cats with different paws raised or one with both held aloft.

Traditionally, the lucky cat is plain white or white spotted with black and orange. However, many colours are available and each has a different function: red ones are said to prevent illness; black wards off evil; blue cats represent academic success; pink ones stimulate romance and enhance business partnerships.

Lucky cats are usually found on counters, at chest level. They should not be placed below the waist or on the floor and they should face the main entrance or a doorway.

Column No 170: July 13, 2008

Wood Cures (Touch Wood)

In traditional feng shui, wood represents romance. Thus, to stimulate one's love life, plants can be placed in the sectors that are associated with the appropriate Flying Stars. Cut flowers are not recommended because their wood energy is much weaker, as the blooms expire within a few days. Artificial plants are also considered ineffective as there is no life energy, or living *chi*, present within them. Similarly, wooden furniture is thought of as dead wood in feng shui and therefore does not have any curative effects.

The interactions between the five elements can also be controlled by the presence of wood. For instance, when the stove and sink are directly opposite each other in the kitchen, the fire and water elements clash, manifesting in discord between the home's occupants. Wood can be placed between the two as water produces wood, which then feeds into fire via the productive element cycle.

Instead of using plants, the colour green can be used to stimulate wood energy. A green mat, for example, should suffice in this regard.

Be wary of placing wood in certain sectors of your home as it may stimulate aggressive energy associated with lawsuits and arguments. Nor should plants be placed in bedrooms, as the associated yang energy will cause insomnia, anxiety and fatigue for the occupants.

Column No 171: July 20, 2008

Fire Cures (Let There Be Light)

When the fire energy within your living space needs to be stimulated, it is advisable not to use actual fire or burn candles. Apart from the safety aspect, such fire cures are considered temporary.

Some feng shui masters believe the ash they produce will simulate the earth element instead. Nowadays, fire energy is introduced through the use of incandescent lighting. This may explain why masters recommend leaving a light on for certain periods of time in a specific sector. However, fluorescent lighting does not contain fire energy.

Colours such as orange, red, yellow, purple, pink and burgundy can be used to represent the fire elements. Apart from painting your walls or pillars in these colours, they can also be incorporated into furniture or soft furnishings such as carpets and cushions. Artwork featuring these hues can also produce the desired effect.

Fire is used to reduce the negative wood energy associated with arguments and lawsuits. It can also stimulate positive and negative forms of earth energy, such as wealth and sickness, depending on which sector it is located in. An excess of fire in the wrong sector, even in the form of colour, may increase the incidence of actual fire outbreaks.

Column No 172: July 27, 2008

Earth Cures (Earth Calling)

For the current time period, the earth element represents wealth and prosperity. However, there are also negative aspects, as it can manifest energies associated with illness, accident and mishap. Earth is used to calm the conflict between fire and metal energies, which otherwise result in occupants having lung and breathing difficulties, headaches and skin problems.

Rather than using containers of soil to avoid these problems, it is preferable to use representative colours, such as yellow, beige, brown and other earth tones.

In classical feng shui theory, the current wealth energy, denoted by the Eight Flying Star, is represented by earth. Thus, to stimulate this energy in your living and working space, feng shui consultants will recommend incorporating earth colours or objects that are made of earth, such as terracotta or clay figures.

Using actual samples of soil may be acceptable in small amounts, but large containers may introduce unwanted health issues.

Compared with fire, earth energy is relatively docile and its placement can also calm the sector that contains the infamous Five-Yellow Flying Star energy, which results in accidents and mishaps.

Column No 173: August 3, 2008

Metal Cures (Heavy Metal)

Metal objects are commonly recommended by feng shui masters as they are used to reduce the negative earth energies associated with illness and accidents. In the cycle of production, metal is formed from earth, thereby reducing its power.

The purer and heavier the metal, the greater its effectiveness in absorbing negative earth energy. While gold and silver would be ideal, their cost sometimes precludes them from being used. Copper can also be considered, and iron is an acceptable alternative, and much more effective than brass or aluminium.

Traditionally, feng shui masters have recommended the use of metal wind chimes and metal Chinese coins. For instance, five old Chinese coins (tied together with red string) can be placed under your mat or can be placed along the edge of your door to reduce the Five-Yellow earth energy there.

A wind chime with six rods is used to contain the Two-Black illness energy, and two and six are believed to form a pair, according to the theory of the *I Ching* trigrams. These days, statues, light fittings and even gadgets can be used to represent metal energy.

Grey and white are the colours that represent metal; those who are not keen to have metallic objects displayed prominently in their home can incorporate these hues into their interior design.

Column No 174: August 10, 2008

Water Cures (Go with the Flow)

The use of water is commonly misunderstood by readers of feng shui books. For instance, having a fountain at the entrance to a home does not automatically confer wealth. Similarly, placing one to the right of the entrance as you look out does not mean your spouse will indulge in extra-marital affairs.

Rather, it is the sector it is placed in (relative to the centre of your home) that determines a water feature's effect. In the productive cycle, water is produces wood. Hence, placing it in the romance sectors associated with wood and water energies will increase the likelihood of romantic developments.

Placing it in a sector that contains your home's wealth energy will also increase your earning potential. This may or may not correspond to the position of the main entrance to your home.

You do not need to keep a water feature flowing all day. Leaving it on for a few hours when someone is at home will suffice. However, the feature should always be in operating order and should not run dry. Ensure the water does not become stagnant and become a breeding ground for mosquitoes and other insects.

For those not keen on having a water feature in their home, colours that represent the element, such as black and blue, can be incorporated into the interior design instead.

Column No 175: August 17, 2008

Money Frogs (Toads to Riches)

You may have come across figurines of three-legged money frogs or toads near the main entrance of homes or shops. Some of these frogs have coins between their lips and some do not; either way they are meant to improve the financial prospects of occupants.

They should be placed next to or inside the front door, preferably in a corner on the floor. A frog with a coin in its mouth should face in towards your home; this way, it will take the wealth inside.

Those with empty mouths should face outwards, attracting opportunities for the inhabitants. Some feng shui masters suggest having a frog face outwards during the day, then turning it inwards at night.

Having a larger frog does not mean you will become more wealthy. You may have seen large money frogs in commercial properties such as restaurants, but these are likely to be in proportion to the size of the premises.

Also getting more money frogs does not result in an increase of fortune.

Be aware that money frogs are merely symbols of wealth. Placing them in your home does not guarantee financial success; they are no substitute for hard work and sound investments.

Column No 186: November 2, 2008

Vases (Pots of Money and Love)

Some feng shui masters recommend placing a vase in the wealth sector of home, in which you keep small pieces of jewellery to symbolise your family's prosperity.

Others suggest half filling the vase with rice or soil and burying coins in it to imply that the occupants will always enjoy wealth and prosperity.

Of course, the traditional use of vases - for flowers - is also beneficial in feng shui. Place a certain number of flowers in a vase in the romance sector of your home to improve love life.

The number of flowers you should display depends on your year of birth. You should keep the water clean and replace dying flowers. Avoid artificial blooms as they have no life force or energy.

Vases should not be left totally empty as this implies that the occupants' fortunes – in wealth or romance - will dry up or disappear. If a vase is badly damaged, it should be replaced; vases can be repaired but any visible cracks bode ill for the occupants.

Column No 199: February 15, 2009

Animal Charms

To avoid misfortune and bad luck during a lunar year, you should wear an animal pendant that will complement the animal of your year of birth.

Those born in the Year of the Rat should carry an ox and vice versa. Tigers will benefit from wearing a pig pendant, while rabbits should match up with dogs. Other pairs include the dragon and rooster, the snake and monkey and the horse and sheep.

The pairs are derived from the Eight Characters of Birth (*paht chee*) school of Chinese astrology. There are other, more complex, calculations involved in this school of astrology that will identify animals that can improve your love life, wealth or luck or have the potential to be your mentor.

Even though the practice of wearing pendants is popular, it has aroused controversy. Some modern feng shui practitioners feel that it is a marketing tool that takes advantage of the trust and gullibility of believers. Such criticism is unfair as this practice has a long history and is undeniably ingrained the culture and psyche of the Chinese people.

Column No 200: February 22, 2009

Artificial Flowers (Flowers of Romance)

The role of artificial flowers in feng shui is a controversial topic. Some masters feel that since they were not present when classical feng shui principles were established, they should not be considered at all.

Then there are those who feel that artificial flowers lack life force, or *chi*, and should be avoided at all costs. One thing is for certain, synthetic flowers should not be used in traditional feng shui formulas to stimulate romance by stimulating the wood energy in an environment. When trying to enhance your love life, there is no substitute for fresh-cut flowers. Even fake flowers that are made of wood should be discounted. A specific number of fresh flowers can be placed in the appropriate sector of a home based on the occupant's birth data. Wilting flowers should always be replaced.

Synthetic flowers do not exert any negative effects but they should always be kept clean. If they are damaged or if their colour has faded, they should be discarded.

It is generally agreed that neither preserved nor shriveled flowers (including wedding bouquets) are considered to have positive energy and they should not be displayed within your home. Images of dead flowers in print form will also increase yin energy, leading to increased incidences of melancholia and depression.

Column No 206: April 5, 2009

Chapter 8

Doors and Windows

The Front Door

This is vital in feng shui because it is the portal through which chi, or energy, enters our homes. Ideally, the front door should open into a hall or living room, allowing chi to circulate and meander through the living space.

Should the front door open directly facing the back door, a balcony or window, chi entering your home rushes straight out again. This is usually seen in apartments where the balcony, affording breathtaking views, lies in a straight line with the front door. The failure to accumulate chi translates into an inability to hold onto one's wealth, hence dwindling savings, or worse, spiraling debt.

One should avoid moving into residences with this feng shui taboo. Otherwise, the problem can be rectified by placing a solid screen (preferably wood or metal, not frosted glass) between the two portals. You can also use blinds or curtains to cover the exposed area directly opposite the front door. Positioning these barriers prevents positive energy leaking out, thereby improving your financial situation.

A client of mine installed a wooden screen between his front door and balcony. Shortly afterwards, his once stagnant copywriting business was swamped with new clients. Feng shui or pure coincidence? You decide.

Column No 3: March 20, 2005

What Lies Outside Your Front Door (On the Doorstep)

In Hong Kong, most of us live in apartments and are unable to exert much control over the structures that lie directly outside our front door. Hence, it is extremely important to ensure that there are no attacking structures outside your main entrance before you move into your home. The positive effects of good internal feng shui will be nullified should the external feng shui be negative or aggressive.

The front door should not lie at the end of a long corridor or passageway; otherwise there will be an increased incidence of health problems and mishaps. There will be similar problems should one's entrance be located directly opposite the lift. Occupants' health will also be adversely affected if there is a fire extinguisher or hose that is directly opposite the main entrance

It's best to avoid living in units with main entrances having these feng shui afflictions. Some feng shui masters suggest placing a mirror above the front door to push back the attacking structures. Having your neighbour's door directly opposite yours will result in a distant relationship because there is competition for positive chi, but it's best to maintain civility and not place any mirrors aimed directly at their entrance. Seek professional help should you discover a mirror aimed directly at you from one of your neighbours.

Column No 8: April 24, 2005

What Lies Outside Your Window (Room With A View)

According to feng shui, the view from a bedroom or living room window is crucial because unfavourable environmental features visible outside may affect a person's health adversely.

Negative environmental features include jagged mountains (naturally occurring or man made) and the sharp edges on buildings. These features give off attacking energy or *sha chi* that will affect a living space, especially if considerable amounts of time are spent in view of them. Other features can be the cutting edge of roads and flyovers, electrical poles, transmission towers and water tanks. Sharp edges of buildings refer to the pointed areas at the corners of buildings; and the sharper the corner, the greater the amount of *sha chi*.

One of the most unfavourable situations would be to have a narrow 'wind tunnel' gap between two buildings opened directly opposite your window or door. Also known as Heaven's Crack, this focus of sharp, attacking energy will definitely create health and wealth problems.

If a window overlooks an unfavourable feature drawing the curtains may help reduce the impact. A mirror placed to reflect back the attacking feature is also thought to help. However, the best solution would be to avoid moving into a residence with such views.

Column No 14: June 5, 2005

Your Front Door (In And Out)

The front door is one of the most important structures in residential feng shui, being the main portal allowing people and chi to enter and exit the home. The size of the front door should be directly proportional to the size of the living space.

The front door should not be too big for a studio apartment, otherwise all the energy within the home will seep out when the door is open, resulting in financial problems. Conversely, if the door is too small for a spacious three bedroom unit, new opportunities may be difficult to come by.

Ideally, the front door should be made up of solid material, such as wood, which not only ensures privacy, but also ensures the home's energy stays within. Translucent, frosted or stained glass may be more aesthetically pleasing to some, but it should not exceed one-third of the total area of your main entrance. A front door made of glass and wire mesh is not recommended.

With regard to the colour of the front door, it is better to seek professional advice because calculations are needed. Suffice it to say, painting your front door red is not necessarily a good thing. Then again, if a neighbour's door has been painted black, he or she will definitely have health problems. The front door is one of the most frequented sectors in the home, never take it for granted.

Column No 22: July 31, 2005

Stairs (Step By Step)

For those living in apartments, having a front door directly opposite the common stairs of a building will create problems. Should the front door of a unit open to a pair of descending staircases, the occupants will have financial problems.

When the front door leads directly to stairs that ascend, there is an increased incidence of accidents and mishaps involving the residents. This is related to the sharp energy associated with the stairs directly overwhelming the front door.

If you live in one of these units, install screens inside your apartment parallel to your front door to shield off the negative energy. If there are space constraints, some feng shui masters suggest using a red rug or mat to control the attacking energy.

For those living in a house, having the stairs lead directly to the front door will result in finances being drained. This is because chi within the house will rush straight out of the front door when it is opened. If possible, redirect the last few steps of the stairs to face away from the front door. If this is not possible, try placing a screen or curtains to block the energy running out.

Avoid moving into or buying properties where the stairs lead directly to the front door.

Column No 39: November 27, 2005

Back Door (Watch Your Back)

In any living space, the back door should be no larger than the front door, otherwise all the energy and opportunities that enter through the main entrance may flow out through the secondary entrance.

Occupants with homes in which the front and back doors lie directly opposite each other will encounter similar problems. When the back door lies in line with the front door, it will create the 'two front doors' phenomenon. There will be arguments and discord between family members; one should block and/or refrain from using the back door in this instance.

A feng shui master may suggest occupants use the back door instead of the front, so as to tap their best directions or the wealth sector. While this controversial practice may be appealing in theory, note any potential benefits may be negated if the occupants' daily routines become severely disrupted.

Several feng shui masters will tell you that having a back door is essential as it allows depleted energy to exit a home. For those who live in apartments without a back door, the main window can act as a substitute and should be left open from time to time. Finally, the back door should be able to open to its full extent; don't clutter the entrance with stacks of unwanted items.

Column No 69: July 9, 2006

Screens (Screen Saver)

In a traditional Chinese house, the front door might open onto a screen adorned with various motifs and images. Not only does a screen afford a degree of privacy for the occupants, it also allows energy to meander from the front door to the rest of the home. The space constraints of modern living preclude screens from being a feature in many homes, but there are several situations that call for them.

If the front entrance lies directly opposite the back door, a balcony, stairs or prominent windows, placing a screen in between will prevent positive energy rushing out of the home. Ideally, the screen should be solid and opaque - preferably wooden, but translucent Japanese-style screens using wax paper are also effective.

Screens can also be used in work areas where one is sitting with one's back against the same wall that shares the entrance. A screen shielding the door will ensure those who enter have to walk past the barrier before turning into the room, thereby allowing the person inside to see who is entering.

Screens can also be used in a bedroom to block the flow of negative energy towards a bed that is in the path of the toilet door. Should there be insufficient space, alternatives such as curtains can also be used.

Column No 71: July 23, 2006

Awkward Doors (Door Ways)

Curtains can be an unobtrusive remedy to awkward door arrangements when there are space constraints preventing the use of a screen. For instance, if your home has three doors located in a straight line – say, the front, hall and bedroom doors - then energy will rush through to the bedroom, which may cause the occupants to suffer insomnia. Hanging a curtain on the second door - thereby simulating a solid wall - will prevent the energy from travelling in a straight line and allow it to circulate instead. The curtains need to be opaque; see-through curtains will not have the desired effect.

Toilet doors that open into inconvenient places, such as adjacent to the front door, kitchen, dining room or living room, or next to the bed in the bedroom, can also be made less obtrusive through the use of curtains. Keeping the toilet door closed is not sufficient.

Depending on the orientation and age of the home, a feng shui consultant will be able to advise on the colour of the curtain as dictated by which of the five elements (water, wood, metal, earth and fire) need to be present.

Keeping the curtains drawn on windows opposite the front door will also prevent energy from rushing out. If a back door directly faces the main entrance, install a curtain rail with thick curtains on the back door.

Column No 72: July 30, 2006

Windows (The Eyes Have It)

In feng shui, the door represents the mouth of a home and the windows its eyes. Having a front door that does not open properly equates to having a blocked mouth and means the home's occupants may find opportunity difficult to come by. Windows left unwashed - including those that require a window cleaner - will lead the residents to make poor decisions and suffer from a lack of foresight. Windows that are broken or cracked may cause eye problems.

Among family members, doors represent parents while windows are the children. The window-to-door ratio should not exceed 30 percent, otherwise there may be disputes between parents and children. There will also be an excess of yang energy, which will exacerbate the tension. The imbalance may be addressed by keeping curtains drawn on certain windows, thereby transforming them into walls.

It's better to have windows that open outward (signifying expanding opportunities) rather than inward (suggesting a lack of confidence). Windows that are too narrow relative to the living space will lead a home's occupants to lack vision.

Homes with windows that only open halfway may encourage their residents to give others false impressions of themselves. Sliding windows should be able to be fully opened, otherwise obstacles will be encountered.

Column No 75: August 20, 2006

External Poison Arrows (Getting to the Point)

You may have come across the term 'poison arrow' in feng shui articles but never grasped its meaning. In classical feng shui, 'poison arrow' refers to the sharp edge of a structure that is aimed directly at another and is thereby 'attacking' it. The term *sha chi* refers to the aggressive energy that is so generated.

Looking out of the front door of your home or building, examples of poison arrows would be straight roads or paths that are heading towards you, the sheer edge of a road as it veers off in another direction and the sharp edges of neighbouring buildings.

When the entrance of a building or residence is exposed to the *sha chi* of poison arrows, potentially negative energy that was previously dormant may be activated, resulting in a higher incidence of accidents, miscommunication and even fires

To rectify the situation, try to relocate your front door, if it is in the path of a poison arrow. Some feng shui masters recommend placing *ba gua* mirrors above (but not on) your main entrance to reflect the negative energy. Where roads are directed straight at buildings, one can place a barrier in front of the entrance to block the *sha chi*. If you live or work in an afflicted building, it may be best to consult a feng shui professional.

Column No 79: September 17, 2006

Slanted Doors (Entry-Level Beliefs)

You may have noticed that the main entrances to some homes and offices are set at an angle. This is a technique used by certain feng shui masters to tap the positive energy from a specific direction, to improve the ability of the occupants to generate wealth.

Every structure is oriented in a certain direction. For instance, if the back wall of a home faces south, the chances are the main door will open to the north.

However, taking into account the time at which a structure was built may not reveal that the direction in which the door opens is not auspicious. It may even bring forth sickness and mishap. In such a case, the master would suggest that the door be angled, so those entering the premises can bring in with them beneficial energy.

Some feng shui masters argue that slanting the door by a few degrees will change the orientation of a structure and the overall nature of the property. This is not so. What is most important is the direction in which the back wall is aligned.

Other experts believe the door should be tilted to suit the year of birth of the occupants (you can imagine how troublesome it would be if every time a property was sold, its door had to be realigned) and there are those who feel that having the main entrance at an angle is detrimental, as a small focus of unsettled energy will build up at the entrance, adversely affecting the health and well-being of the occupants.

Column No 181: September 28, 2008

Apartments with Views (High Risks)

Apartments on higher floors, and therefore with better views, are generally more valuable than those closer to the ground. However, from a feng shui perspective, having a better view does not necessarily translate into better fortune.

For instance, if your front door opens onto a balcony that offers those spectacular vistas, energy will rush straight out, making it difficult for you to hold on to money. Also, you should not work at a desk facing a window because you will be distracted.

Placing your bed so that the sunrise is the first thing you see when you wake up may sound good in theory. But if the head of your bed is against the wall that backs onto the toilet of an en suite bathroom or if you have your back to the bedroom door you will have problems.

Finally, consider that when you become accustomed to spectacular views, they will take on the quality of wallpaper – they will lose their appeal. Opting for a unit with a better design may ultimately prove more beneficial.

Column No 207: April 12, 2009

Chapter 9

Exteriors

Car Parks (Engine Trouble)

In Hong Kong, many of us live in buildings that have underground car parks. The pollution from the cars means that our living environment should be kept separate from this area, and it is recommended that you do not live in units situated directly above car parks. Sleeping above this hollow space gives residents a feeling of instability, which is why it's better to live in flats on higher floors because there is more support.

You should also try to avoid units that are opposite the entrance to car parks, because the constant rush of energy caused by the arriving and departing cars will upset the feng shui balance in your home. It is not good feng shui to be in the direct path of cars constantly heading either towards or away from you. This introduces excessive yang energy that will make you agitated and impatient.

This situation can be alleviated by drawing the blinds or curtains. But placing symbolic barriers, such as stones on your mantelpiece, will have no effect.

Overlooking a car park from your bedroom window isn't a feng shui problem, especially if it doesn't generate much traffic or if your window is not on the same level as the garage entrance. It is unnecessary to keep your curtains drawn in this situation; overreacting is as ineffective as under reacting.

Column No 17: June 26, 2005

146

Water In Front, Mountain Behind (River Deep, Mountain High)

One of the most positive feng shui layouts is having mountains behind and water flowing in front of your home, an ideal situation that feng shui masters have always sought. For city dwellers, surrounding buildings fulfil the role of mountains, while roads (with moving traffic) replace water.

Does this mean having buildings behind you and a road in front will immediately denote good feng shui? Not necessarily. Just as traditional feng shui masters assessed the quality of mountains, you will need to consider the nature of neighbouring buildings. If the building behind you is significantly smaller than yours, there won't be much support provided.

Conversely, if the building behind you is extremely tall and presses down on yours, there will be problems. Ideally, the building behind should be wider and taller to provide support. Any roads in front of your building should not be highways or roads that are always jammed with traffic. Ideally, they should cradle your building and not run straight at or cut into it.

According to more complex formulas, about 25 per cent of buildings benefit from having mountains in front and water behind, but you need a professional to assess which ones do and which ones do not.

Column No 37: November 13, 2005

Tall and Short Buildings (Building Tension)

When assessing an apartment unit, feng shui masters consider not only the interior; they also take into account the overall environment of the apartment building.

For instance, if the tallest apartment block within a cluster of buildings protrudes significantly from the rest, it is considered a lonely building that lacks protection from its neighbours. Its isolated position also exposes it to strong winds, which further prevents positive *chi* from accumulating. Those living in such buildings will feel as if they have no support and may also be prone to betrayal by others.

When the surrounding blocks dwarf a building, it is considered overwhelmed by others. Overwhelmed structures include those that are significantly smaller than the one opposite, such as a two-storey building that has a tall apartment block opposite. A 40-floor tower behind a 30-storey building will confer protection to the structure in front, but a 40-floor tower behind a five-storey block overpowers it. Those living in buildings that are dwarfed will constantly feel frustrated as they may encounter setbacks.

For those living in 'lonely' or pressured buildings, relocation may be an option. Note that construction of other buildings of similar height in the vicinity will provide support for the lonely building, thereby improving its feng shui.

Column No 76: August 27, 2006

Buildings to Avoid (Building Woes)

The overall proportion, design and shape of a residential or commercial block will invariably affect those who work or live within it. For favourable feng shui, the length, breadth and height of any building should all be in proportion.

Blocks that are extremely tall and narrow will give their occupants feelings of insecurity. Those living or working in buildings that are cantilevered (where the ground floor is smaller than the floors above) will suffer financial losses and experience difficulties in initiating projects.

Another feng shui situation to avoid is when two tall buildings sandwich a smaller building, and thereby overwhelm the one that is significantly shorter. The occupants of the building in the middle will feel disillusioned with their lives and may develop feelings of inferiority.

'Heaven's gap' opens up when a wind tunnel is created by the narrow gap between two high-rise buildings. Attacking *chi* accumulates and subsequently flows into any buildings that lies directly opposite it. Those living in a block directly opposite such a gap will be subject to extremely sharp energy and will be prone to mishaps and accidents. It's best to avoid occupying buildings in such a position.

Column No 77: September 3, 2006

Electricity (Power Corrupts)

Feng Shui practitioners believe living in close proximity to electricity transmission pylons and substations can have undesirable consequences. For instance, people living in buildings near high-voltage pylons may suffer emotional imbalances and physical illness due to the electromagnetic *chi* they emit. Similarly, people living near telecommunication towers may have an increased incidence of nervous disorders while those residing in industrial zones could be prone to respiratory problems.

People who can see electricity pylons in the distance from their homes should not worry; the structures need to be significant in size and nearby to have any impact.

Some feng shui masters think electricity substations represent the fire element and may prove beneficial for occupants. However, it is still undesirable to have them directly opposite one's front door, or to live immediately next to them, because of the toxic energy they produce.

To counteract the fire of such fixtures, experienced feng shui masters use water. The location and position of water is determined by calculations involving the age and orientation of a property. However, it is still best to avoid moving into homes that are close to emitters of electromagnetism.

Column No 84: October 22, 2006

Roads (On the Road)

In traditional feng shui, the flow and shape of water (for example, a river) around a property is seen as exerting positive or negative effects as a constant flow equates to yang energy. In modern city living, roads have replaced waterways in their significance, so you should note the shape of roads in your building's vicinity.

For instance, when a road curves, it's preferable to be on the inner, or embracing side, rather than the outer. When your building is on the embracing side, it is described in classical texts as being akin to wearing a jade belt around your waist, implying protection and prosperity.

If your property is on the outside edge, it is exposed to sharp energy, resulting in adversity for the occupants. Because these features are structural, it's best to avoid moving into a home that suffers from them.

You should also avoid buildings at the end of intersections or T junctions, as you will be exposed to sharp incoming energy. Installing a solid barrier around the front entrance of the building will provide some protection.

Some traditional feng shui masters use a solid rock inscribed with the face of a lion or tiger and calligraphy to control the incoming energy, but the surrounding architecture and the beliefs of occupants also need to be considered.

Column No 93: December 24, 2006

Bridges (A Bridge Too Far)

You should avoid living in buildings that are near bridges used by heavy traffic because the excessive yang energy generated may cause occupants anxiety and headaches. If your building is next to a flyover, it's best to avoid living in the units immediately beside or below the traffic. Units several floors above a bridge or flyover won't be so affected.

It's also not advisable to live in units that are at the same level as overhead pedestrian bridges, especially if your balcony or window aligns with the pathway across such a structure. In this case, you should install a barrier, such as a row of plants or a solid screen, between your unit and the 'attacking' structure.

Another configuration to avoid is the Y junction: when a building is between two converging bridges or roads. It's also known as the scissors junction, as it resembles the mouth of a pair of scissors. There is a greater incidence of traffic accidents due to the sharp and excessive yang energy that's generated at these junctions. Occupants will also be more prone to mishaps.

Traditionally, feng shui masters use a stone tablet inscribed with the Chinese characters for "Tai Shan mountain resisting stone" to counter the negative energy; the rock will prevent the two ends of the 'scissors' from coming together.

Column No 94: January 7, 2007

Trees (Trees of Knowledge)

The amount of greenery in your neighbourhood is a good indication of the chi that is present. If trees and plants are thriving, this indicates the presence of positive energy. Conversely, avoid moving to an area where the lawn in the compound/park or the plants in the balcony don't seem to grow well, as there might be a significant amount of *shar*, or negative *chi*.

If trees and plants grow away rather than towards a property, this suggests that the building in question may contain unhealthy energy.

There should not be any trees in the direct path of the entrance of your building as this may result in occupants encountering obstacles in their lives. Feng Shui masters do not advocate chopping down healthy trees; it is best to replant the tree in a more appropriate location. Having multiple trees obscuring the entrance of your property also creates an excess of yin energy, which contributes to residents feeling lethargic and melancholic.

Should there be dead or withered trees near your property, excessive yin energy will be generated. Shrivelled trees are also an indicator of decline and should be removed. It's best to consult a feng shui professional who will also advise on the most appropriate time to uproot and destroy a dead tree.

Column No 95: January 14, 2007

Surroundings (Neighbourhood Watch)

Regardless of where you live, be it an apartment block or a villa, the surrounding buildings affect the feng shui of your property. It's preferable to live in an area that is purely residential, without significant commercial or industrial activity because these can adversely affect your physical and psychological health.

You should also avoid living in properties adjacent to buildings associated with illness and death. Living next to hospitals, clinics and nursing homes may expose you to yin energy that will leave you lethargic. Maternity hospitals are problematic because of the pain associated with childbirth, while mortuaries and funeral homes produce energy associated with grief. If you live in a unit with windows that open onto public toilets or rubbish bins, your health will be adversely affected and you should move.

Excessively yang buildings, such as police stations, law courts, jails and military barracks, should be avoided because of the aggression and arguments that occur within them. Living near these places could cause you to be nervous and irritable.

Some feng shui masters advise against living opposite schools because the extremes of yang and yin energy (during school time and after hours) can cause agitation.

Column No 96: January 21, 2007

Off the Plans (The Personal Touch)

Technological advances such as GPS and satellite imaging made available through the internet have brought clarity and convenience in our lives, but they play a limited role in a traditional feng shui assessment of a property.

While a building's exact location can be pinpointed, it is difficult to provide a three-dimensional picture of the surrounding environment, such as the shape and size of neighbouring buildings and structures, both natural (trees) and man-made (street signs).

Nothing compares to the feng shui consultant being able to observe the physical environment and measure the orientation with a Chinese *luo pan* or even a western compass.

It is extremely difficult, if not impossible, for feng shui masters to conduct a thorough assessment solely from plans submitted via fax or the internet. A professional and competent consultant would never request clients provide a detailed plan for appraisal as any mistakes in the drawings would affect the accuracy of calculations.

Feng Shui masters also caution clients against buying apartments off the plan because unexpected changes to the layout, orientation and surroundings could adversely affect a property's feng shui. After all, even the best-laid plans can go awry.

Column No 97: January 28, 2007

External Changes (Life is a Rollercoaster)

You may have heard it said that feng shui is 'cyclical', which suggests a person's good or bad feng shui will be subject to changes and fluctuations. A residence that previously enjoyed good feng shui may see a sudden reversal in fortune.

So what are the factors contributing to the alterations in one's luck? Regardless of whether you are living in an apartment or house, any changes to the exterior of your home, some of which may be well beyond your control, will affect it.

For instance, the building's management may install a fire extinguisher or hose directly opposite the entrance to your apartment, thereby sending attacking energy towards your front door. Or, if the neighbouring unit or plot is unoccupied for a significant period of time, this could lead to an excessive accumulation of yin energy, which could adversely affect your health.

While new buildings in your neighbourhood will introduce positive yang energy, be wary if these buildings have sharp corners aimed towards your home or block your view. If you walk out onto your balcony only to be in the shadow cast by a new building, you may have to reconsider relocating.

Column No 138: November 19, 2007

Mountains (Mountain Concerns)

You may have heard that it is good, in feng shui terms, to have mountains behind your home. While this is true, you should also take into account the quality of the mountains. Those that are lush with plenty of plants and trees are preferable to those that are barren or have been damaged by construction or mining.

Mountains that have sustained such damage are known as 'wounded dragons' and are sources of *sha chi* or negative energy. Mountains with jagged edges are also considered negative. Avoid moving into areas in front of such ranges as there is no remedy to sufficiently protect you from these effects.

Even if you live on an extremely green hill or mountain, it is preferable that you don't live right at the top, as this will leave you feeling vulnerable. It is better to live halfway up, as you will have support from behind and shelter from strong winds.

The position and direction of mountains relative to your property should also be noted. There are certain formulas in classical feng shui, inscribed on traditional compasses, that advise on the best relative locations.

Column No 190: November 30, 2008

Chapter 10

Feng Shui Calculations

Wealth Position (Wealth of Knowledge)

Several formulas can be used to determine the wealth position (*choy wai*) in a home that take into account an individual's astrological data, such as when the home was built and the current year. The most direct and commonly used method of identifying the wealth position is to locate the area diagonally opposite the front door.

Depending on the position of the front door, a home may have more than one wealth sector. There should not be any windows in the wealth sector, as wealth will flow out of them. Windows adjacent to the wealth sector(s) should have their curtains drawn to keep wealth in. Alternatively, you can also place plants or furniture adjacent to these sectors to prevent chi from the front door flowing out.

Some feng shui masters suggest placing water features, such as aquariums, or symbols of wealth, such as the *choy mao* or wealth cat, in these corners.

Keep in mind there are more complex calculations involved in identifying the wealth position. There is no one fixed wealth sector (i.e. the South East) that can be applied to all homes. Traditional feng shui is not that simple.

Column No 12: May 22, 2005

The Compass (Compass Points)

Chances are you might have noticed the Chinese feng shui compass, or *luo pan*. In Hong Kong, and in Chinatowns in other cities, smaller versions of it can be seen hanging on or above doors, and it is widely available for sale in Chinese markets. What is its significance?

Luo means to encompass all types of information from various sources, while *pan* refers to a plate. In other words, the compass is a collection of plates that encodes theories from numerous feng shui schools. It comes in two parts, the basic free-standing wooden saucer-shaped disc, or the functional form, with the circular disc fitting and rotating within a square wooden base, marked with two sighting lines made of red thread.

All compasses have a central area enclosed in glass where a magnetised needle is suspended in methylated spirits and rotates to align itself with north and south. Traditionally, feng shui masters are able to determine from the alignment of the compass needle the direction of the property they are assessing.

Apart from being the feng shui master's tool, the *luo pan* is also used to protect against negative, or *sha*, energy, which explains why it is sometimes hung vertically above front doors.

Column No 23: August 7, 2005

Directions (The Way Forward)

The direction certain elements in the home face play a vital role in feng shui. For example, it is uncommon to see north-facing doors in traditional Chinese homes as this exposed them to cold winter winds. There are also rules governing the direction faced by the front door, stove and bed.

There are four cardinal directions: north, south, east and west, and four inter-cardinal directions in between them: northeast, northwest, southeast and southwest. With 360 degrees on the compass, each of the eight cardinal and inter-cardinal directions has a 45-degree range. To the casual observer these parameters may be sufficient but not for feng shui professionals, who further subdivide each of the eight directions into three sectors, giving us a total of 24 'sub-directions', each with a range of 15 degrees. This means that north can be broken down into north-one, north-two and north-three.

When it comes to detailed feng shui calculations, there is a difference between north-one, which lies in the western boundary of north, compared to north-three, which is at the eastern boundary.

Simply telling the feng shui consultant that your house sits in the north without telling him which sector it is in will be insufficient for a detailed assessment.

Column No 107: April 15, 2007

162

Taking A Reading (The Right Direction)

If you have been present at a professional feng shui consultation, you will have seen the master using the traditional feng shui compass, or *luo pan* to determine the orientation of the home or front door.

Some consultants stand in the centre of the home to measure the facing direction, but the problem with this approach is that for irregularly shaped properties it is difficult, if not impossible, to determine the centre with precision.

An easier approach would be to stand with your back parallel to your front door while holding a compass and look outwards. If using a western compass, hold it anywhere between the chest and waist; a *luo pan* should be held at waist height. Ensure your back is at a slight distance from, and not in direct contact with, the door.

Remove any metallic watches, belts or jewellery, as this may affect the accuracy of the reading. There are also external environmental features that may interfere with the reading, such as metallic doors, adjacent lift shafts and electric wires or boxes. To reduce such interference, move away from the front door until the needle settles.

Column No 108: April 22, 2007

Practical Directions (All Over the Place)

Apart from determining which direction faces, there are other issues to consider: for instance, the orientation in which direction you sleep. This is determined by the way your head – not your feet – points when you lie in your bed.

In the kitchen, feng shui masters assess the position of the stove from the wall behind it. Don't assume the direction of a cooker is determined by orientation of its knobs as these can be on a different plane. Measuring the direction in which an electrical cord exits your rice cooker, kettle or microwave oven has no basis in classical feng shui, so don't place kitchen appliances in impractical positions to tap favourable 'cable' directions.

With regard to favourable sitting positions, when at your desk or dining table, some masters emphasise the direction in which you face, while others place credence on your position at the table. Regardless of which theory you follow, it is most important to consider features such as doors, windows or passageways and avoid sitting with them behind you.

Keep everything in perspective. There's no need to be so concerned with directions that, for example, you worry about which way your toilet faces.

Column No 109: April 29, 2007

Direction and Location (Seeking Direction)

Stand in front of a door or a wall with a feng shui compass and you should be able to ascertain the orientation (*fong xiong*) of the wall, or the direction in which the front door faces. In feng shui, another unit of measurement is the sector, or *fong wai*, e.g. the northeast sector.

To differentiate between orientation, direction and location, it helps to think of the former as a two dimensional line and the latter as a three dimensional space, i.e. you might sit facing north at your dining table while the dining room itself is in the eastern sector of your home.

The simplest way to distinguish between the various sectors of the home is to have a plan in front of you and divide the length of your property into three equal portions. Having done that, you divide the breadth of your living space into three equal parts, thereby giving you nine parts in total. Next, identify where north lies and place it in the corresponding one of the nine boxes. The box that lies directly opposite will be south.

The remaining six sectors can then be marked out with the central box denoting the centre of the home.

This principle can also be applied, on a smaller scale, to your bedroom and office. It may also help to associate various sectors with pieces of furniture to aid visualisation.

Column No 110: May 6, 2007

Directional Formulas (The Lie of the Land)

The Eight Mansions formula is the one most commonly used by feng shui masters to determine the direction one should face when sleeping or sitting. It divides people into two groups – east and west.

To determine which group a person belongs to, the practitioner takes the last two digits of their birth year and uses them to come up with a figure between one and nine. For example, 1971 becomes eight (7 + 1) and 1989 also becomes eight (8 + 9 = 17, then 1 + 7 = 8).

That number is then subtracted from 10 for men. For women, five is added. The final figure, called your *kua*, must be between one and nine; if it is higher (as it can be for women), add the two digits together to arrive at the correct *kua*.

You are then classified as an east (if your *kua* is one, three, four or nine) or a west (two, six, seven and eight) person, according to the *I Ching*. Those whose *kua* number is five are given the west number of 2 if they are male, or eight if they are female. Those born in January or February need to use the solar calendar – which begins on February 4 – to determine their year of birth, not the lunar.

Feng Shui consultants relate the *kua* numbers and their elements to various sectors of your home, and do not focus solely on tapping the most favourable direction.

Column No 111: May 13, 2007

166

Directional Formulas II (Face Facts)

Feng Shui masters use astrology to identify favourable directions. The Three Harmony, or *San He*, formula takes into account the Chinese zodiac animal of your year of birth. Each of the 12 animals is associated with a specific direction: for instance, the rat is associated with the north, the horse with the south. You should avoid the animal that clashes with your zodiac sign.

As the rat and the horse clash in the zodiac, those born in the year of the rat should avoid facing the south and those born in the year of the horse should avoid facing the north. Favourable directions come from the animals that are in harmony with, or bring benefit to, your zodiac animal.

A more detailed approach would be to analyse your complete astrological chart - the time, day, month and year of your birth - then identify which of the five elements you lack. Each of the elements is assigned one or more directions: water represents the north, metal the west and northwest and wood the east and southeast.

Those needing more metal should sleep with their head pointing towards the west or northwest. Those with excessive metal in their charts should avoid sleeping or sitting in the metal directions. However, remember that sitting with your back to a door or window will nullify any benefits gained from tapping your favourable directions.

Column No 112: May 20, 2007

167

Family Sectors (Location, Location)

Depending on where they are found, negative external environmental features, such as an oncoming road, and internal flaws, for example, a crack in the wall will have adverse effects on specific inhabitants of a home. The Chinese book of changes, the *I Ching*, contains the Later Heaven Arrangement of the eight trigrams. Each trigram links a specific family member (or a person from a specific age group) with a location.

The northwest represents the father or head of the household and the southwest the mother or head female of the family. These sectors also affect those who are aged 50 and above. For instance, a bachelor in his 50s would be wise to see if there are any structural problems in the northwest sector of his home that might account for any problems he is experiencing.

Family members associated with the north and south are the middle son and the middle daughter, respectively, or men and women aged between 20 and 35.

For those below the age of 20, the relevant sectors are the northeast (for the youngest son) and the west (for the youngest daughter). Men aged between 35 and 50 are affected by the east (the eldest son sector) while women in the same age group are represented by the southeast (the eldest daughter sector).

Column No 113: May 27, 2007

Anatomical Sectors (In Your Element)

Chinese medicine and feng shui have common ground: for example, the concept of yin and yang, and the interaction of the five elements (water, wood, fire, metal and earth). Each of the eight cardinal and inter-cardinal sectors within the home corresponds to one of these elements and therefore to various parts of the body.

The north is associated with the water and thus relates to the kidneys, bladder, urinary tract and the ears. The south corresponds to fire, which represents the heart, circulatory system and the eyes. The earth element is linked to the southwest (yin) and the northeast (yang). The former is associated with the digestive system, the female reproductive system and the spleen, while the latter symbolises the hands, feet, tendons and pancreas.

The east and southeast denote wood, with the yang east signifying the liver, legs and joints, and the yin southeast the gall bladder, thighs and buttocks. The northwest is the yang metal domain, associated with the head, brain, the bones and the spinal column. The yin metal sector lies in the west, and corresponds to the lungs, mouth and skin.

Feng Shui masters can identify which sector has problems (for example, sharp corners on a neighbouring structure) and correlate it to the health of an abode's occupants.

Column No 114: June 3, 2007

169

Wealth Sector (Searching for a Star)

The Flying Star method of feng shui takes into account the element of time and can identify which sector of your home or office is associated with a specific event. The feng shui master can identify the ruling star of the year, which is then placed in the centre of a grid. The eight other stars are then flown into the eight remaining sectors in a fixed clockwise sequence. Because we are now in period eight (which runs until February 2024), the current wealth star is the eighth.

Activity will stimulate the wealth star. If, for example, the wealth sector is in the east, so offices and homes with main entrances in the eastern sector will perform well.

Another method of stimulating the wealth sector is through the placement of water features. However, before doing this, you should take into account what other stars (as determined by the orientation and age of your property) are present, otherwise stars with negative qualities may be accidentally activated.

The wealth star is of the earth element, and placing red and orange objects (representing fire) in its sector will also help stimulate it. Lighting can improve the wealth star, and if it falls into an extremely yin, or shady, room (for example, a storeroom), you may need to consult a feng shui professional to alleviate this problem.

Column No 151: March 2, 2008

Health Sectors (In Sickness and in Health)

According to the Flying Stars method of feng shui, it is important to identify the sickness sector for the year. Let us suppose it is located in the northwest. If the front door of your home or business is located in this sector, there might be an increased incidence of illness and lethargy. However, if you are in the health profession and the sickness star is present at the entrance, it will enhance your business.

Don't be overtly concerned if your bedroom lies in the northwest sector as there are strategies designed to overcome the negative energy. As the sickness star is an earth star, using metallic colours such as white, grey and silver will help to reduce its energy.

This explains why some feng shui masters suggest placing metal wind chimes or coins in the sickness sector. Other alternatives include metal objects such as lamps and sculptures. Note that the greater the weight of the metal, the more effective it will be

In the productive cycle, fire stimulates earth. Thus, using red, burgundy, purple or maroon in the sickness sector will just increase the malignancy of the star.

Column No 152: March 9, 2008

Facing Direction (Right Direction)

You may have heard the terms 'facing direction' and 'sitting direction' used by feng shui professionals. Both terms refer to the overall shape of your apartment and the whereabouts of the main entrance and exit.

The facing direction is where the majority of yang energy enters. Some feng shui masters will take the direction in which the front door faces as the main criterion. Stand at your front door and look out with a compass in your hands. If you face north as you look out, then that is the facing direction of your property.

The sitting direction is 180 degrees from the facing direction, so a north-facing property would be south-sitting. Once the orientation of a home is determined, calculations are then made to determine the various sectors.

For properties that are irregularly shaped (especially apartments), feng shui masters will employ other criteria to assess the sitting and facing directions. These include identifying the main wall, windows and balconies.

It is also overtly simplistic to warn against moving into a property with a certain orientation without taking into account other factors such as when the building was constructed and the astrological data of its occupants.

Column No 158: April 20, 2008

Animal Sectors (Mastering Degrees)

When feng shui masters assess directions, they use units of 15 degrees known as the 24 'Mountains', which are inscribed on Chinese compasses, or *luo pans*. Each of the four cardinal (for example, south or east) and four inter-cardinal directions (such as northwest or southeast) are divided into three units to obtain the 24 Mountains. The 12 zodiac animals account for half of these mountains while the remaining 12 are represented by eight yin and yang element markers and four trigrams of the *I Ching*. The markers include those of water, wood, fire and metal but exclude earth, which symbolises the centre, so it is not ascribed to any direction. The four *I Ching* trigrams indicate the centre of the inter-cardinal sectors, that is, southwest, southeast, northwest and northeast.

Four of the 12 animals indicate the centre of the cardinal directions. For instance, the rat represents north (352.5 to 7.5 degrees) while the horse represents south (172.5 to 187.5 degrees). The other eight animals are assigned to the inter-cardinal directions. For example, the ox represents 22.5 to 37.5 degrees and the tiger 52.5 to 67.5 degrees.

The animal sectors are used to identify directions that should be avoided. For instance, a person should not sleep with their head pointing to or sit with their back to the direction that clashes with their year of birth.

Column No 165: June 8, 2008

Practical Usage of Compass (Get Your Bearings)

The feng shui master traditionally takes readings with their *luo pan* or Chinese feng shui compass. This is an essential tool that provides significantly more information about a person's living or working environment than a standard western compass.

The *luo pan* usually consists of a rotating circular section (which may be black or yellow) enclosed within a square plate (usually red). The centre of the *luo pan*, also known as Heaven's Pool, contains a magnetized needle lying in a circle of methylated spirits that aligns itself to magnetic north-south.

The feng shui master needs to align the central needle with the markings etched at the bottom of the pool. The end of the needle, which rotates to the north, has a central hole with two protrusions on either side.

The feng shui master lines up the top of the needle with the two dots on the base of the pool to determine where north lies. Then the orientation of the property being assessed can be determined.

The effects of surrounding structures, both natural and man made can also be assessed. The feng shui master can use the compass to identify where water should enter and exit your property. This refers to the layout and design of local roads and drains.

Column No 188: November 16, 2008

Buying a Compass (A Few Pointers)

The *luo pan*, or feng shui compass can be used for both practical and decorative purposes. They can be made from natural or fibreglass reinforced wood (known as 'electric wood'). Natural wood compasses last longer and have a pleasant feel to them while the fibreglass reinforced versions are weather resistant but heavier. There are versions with a plastic outer layer but these are more susceptible to wear and tear.

Luo pans come in various sizes, the smaller ones being between 6cm and 10.7cm in diameter, the larger being between 15.7cm and 21.8 cm. Note that the smaller compasses aren't as accurate as the larger models, which tend to be used by feng shui practitioners.

When buying a *luo pan*, check the integrity of the central needle; it should rotate easily but once it is aligned along the north-south axis, it should stay fixed. Reject any *luo pans* with needles that move after they have been aligned.

Those with a circular plate laid out on a square plate should be able to rotate freely with slight resistance. The inscriptions on the layers should also be clearly legible. Those with faded characters should only be used for ornamental purposes.

Column No 189: November 23, 2008

175

More Health Problems (Organ Rhythms)

Feng Shui shares the same principles as Chinese medicine in terms of the five elements, each of which represents a major organ; fire is the heart, water the kidneys, earth the stomach, metal the lungs and wood the liver.

When there is an imbalance of the fire element, you will suffer heart problems. If the stove is in the centre of the home or if the kitchen is beneath a bedroom, occupants may have cardiac issues.

Each of the eight cardinal and inter-cardinal sectors within your home are aligned with family members and body organs. For instance, the north-west sector represents the metal element and consequently the patriarch and the lungs. If this sector is missing or if there is negative energy attacking from dead trees or roads, then the head of the household may be affected or occupants could suffer respiratory problems.

A more complex approach to fixing the problem is to determine the effects exerted by the property's sickness stars, which are calculated from its orientation, time of construction and the current year and month.

The illness star is of the earth element, and if it is present in a bedroom, place metallic objects such as coins, sculptures and lamps in the room to reduce the negative energy. A *wu lou* (gourd or calabash) will also help absorb illness energy.

Column No 196: January 18, 2009

Moving Wealth Sector (Do the Maths)

You may have read that the auspicious, or wealth sector this year lies in a particular direction such as the southeast part of a home. If so then it was in the east sector last year and the west sector the year before that. This raises the questions: why does the wealth sector move from year to year, and what determines that shift?

The moving wealth sector is particular to the Flying Stars School of feng shui, which is popular in Hong Kong. The basis of this theory is that every year there is a different type of energy that governs your home and the world at large.

The energy here refers to the quality of the nine 'Flying Stars', which is considered by some to be a form of Chinese numerology, and by others to be a pattern of chi.

To determine which energy is in control for the year, the first step is to add all four digits of the year together. For 2009, the calculations would be as follows : 2+0+0+9, which gives you 11. You then reduce this number to a number between 1 and 10 (11 = 1+1 which makes 2).

The final step is to subtract this number from 11, (11-2 = 9), a number that is always constant in these calculations. The governing number for 2009 is therefore nine, which denotes the star of celebration and happiness.

For the year 2010, using the same steps as above, the governing number will be eight. The governing number determines the position of certain Flying Stars in a home according to a grid.

Column No 201: March 1, 2009

Pattern of Flight (Flight Paths)

As we have seen, according to the Flying Stars school of feng shui, the governing energy of 2009 is represented by the number nine (as calculated in last week's column). The wealth sector for that year is determined by the location of the number eight, as it has been since 2004, and will be until 2024. Energy associated with the number eight is auspicious.

To determine where the Flying Stars wealth sector is located in a home, you need to 'fly the stars' according to a fixed pattern. First, draw up a naughts-and-crosses grid with nine sections. These sections correspond to the centre, the four cardinal sectors (north, south, east, west) and the four inter-cardinal sectors (i.e. northeast, northwest, southeast, southwest) of a home. For feng shui calculations, north is shown at the bottom of the grid and south at the top, so label all the sectors accordingly.

The fixed order of 'flight' is as follows: centre, northwest, west, northeast, south, north, southwest, east and, finally, south east. In 2009, place nine (representing the governing energy) in the centre and then place one to eight according to the fixed order above (one in the northwest, two in the west etc). The wealth sector, represented by the number eight, thus falls in the southeast sector in your home.

For 2010, the governing number is eight, so the wealth sector will be in the centre of the grid and the centre of your home (nine, the star of celebration and happiness, falls in the northwest sector, one in the west). In 2011, the number will be seven, which means the wealth sector will fall in the northwest.

Column No 202: March 8, 2009

Romance Sector (Spread the Love)

Just because we may be in the Year of the Tiger – an aggressive animal – it does not mean that your chances of romance or marriage will be diminished.

To stimulate romance, focus on the west and north sectors in 2010. This is where the energy associated with romance will be located in 2010, according to the Flying Stars system.

The reason is that the west is where the one-water star will be located in 2010. To improve your chances of romance, place a water feature – a fountain or aquarium - in this sector of your home. The four wood star will be located in the north and this can be stimulated by placing a water feature or plants (but not artificial ones) there.

If the north or west of your apartment is where your bedroom is located, then, to prevent a water feature from interfering with your sleep, place one in the same directional sector of your living room. Water should always be kept clean and functioning.

Of course, feng shui isn't magic. If you stimulate the romance sectors but avoid any social interaction, you won't find love.

Column No 248: January 31, 2010

Grand Duke Theory (Dukes of Hazard)

The Cantonese expression *fan tai sui* translates into English as 'offending the Grand Duke'. This does not mean that one has behaved inappropriately in front of royalty. Rather, *tai sui* refers to one of the 60 gods that make up the sexagenary (60-fold) cycle of years. The full complement of statues of the 60 'Grand Dukes' can be seen in temples dedicated to them in Taiwan and in Hong Kong.

'Grand duke' also refers to the governing Chinese zodiac animal for the year, which, for 2010, is the tiger. Hence, those who offend the Grand Duke this year are those who were born in a Year of the Tiger – 1938, 1950, 1962, 1974, 1986 and 1998. There is the mistaken impression that those born in a Year of the Tiger are destined to have a bad year.

Rather, those who should be more concerned are those who clash with the Grand Duke, such as those born in a Year of the Monkey (1944, 1956, 1968, 1980, 1992 and 2004) which clashes with the Tiger. Some feng shui masters recommend that those born in a clashing year should pay their respects at a temple so as to reduce any potential misfortune. But it is too generalized to assume that all those born under the monkey sign will suffer a bad year.

A more detailed analysis of a person's eight characters of birth, or *paht chee* (as expressed by the time, day, month and year), and his luck cycle will yield more clues.

Column No 251: February 28, 2010

Grand Duke Practical (Building Blocks)

The *tai sui*, or Grand Duke, sector refers to the sector that is governed by the animal sign of the current year. In 2010 it was the tiger, which is located at 52.5 to 67.5 degrees. This corresponds to the northeast sector. Now we know where the Grand Duke sector is, how does that help us?

It is recommended you don't dig, drill or knock down any walls in the Grand Duke sector of your property. Even if this sector of your garden requires some work, you'd be best advised to wait until next year to carry it out.

If you undertake any major renovation in this sector, you are disturbing or moving the Grand Duke, and this may result in financial loss, health problems or accidents and mishaps. If it is imperative for you to carry out some construction in the Grand Duke sector, it is preferable that you consult an experienced feng shui practitioner, who will suggest dates on which to carry out the work to minimise the detrimental effects.

Don't assume that misfortune will occur to all occupants of properties that sit in the Grand Duke sector this year. What is important is that this sector is kept tranquil. If this condition is met, living in, or moving into, a property that sits there in the current year, will not be problematic in terms of feng shui.

Column No 252: March 7, 2010

Chapter 11

Internal Shapes and Structures

Beams and False Ceilings

When sleeping, there should not be any overhanging structures (i.e. lights, overhead fans) above your head or body. Structures that press down on the person will result in health problems. You should relocate the bed or remove the overhanging structure to reduce these negative effects. The same principle also applies to overhanging beams or the edges of uneven ceilings.

Homes with central air conditioning units tend to have uneven ceilings and it would be detrimental to one's health and well being to place beds under the edge made by its ducting.

When the ceiling edge splits your bed in half vertically, your marriage or relationship may be placed in jeopardy. When the ceiling edge runs across the bed horizontally, you should observe which part of the body lies under the edge. A beam that cuts across the head will result in the occupants having headaches, while the edge that presses down upon the occupants' chest will cause lung or heart problems. Reproductive problems may occur when the horizontal structure is above the groin.

If you are unable to relocate your bed, the other option would be to create a false ceiling that is even across its whole width. Placing flutes or other structures that only symbolically push up the beam or structure will not be effective.

Column No 5: April 3, 2005

Floors (On the Level)

Split-level apartments or floors are not advocated by feng shui masters, because the lower levels tend to be focal points of yin energy. For instance, if the dining room is on a lower level than the rest of a home, the occupants may tend to feel lethargic and unmotivated after meals. This can be alleviated by turning up overhead lighting in the area, which increases the overall energy.

Those with wooden floors should not have the boards or planks running parallel to the front door because this suggests obstacles to overcome. Rather, the boards should run from the door into the house, an arrangement that will draw in energy. Abstract and irregular floor designs impart a sense of disorder and confusion, so it's preferable to have balanced, regular and harmonious designs.

Uneven or rocky floor surfaces should be avoided as they imply life won't run smoothly. Prominent cracks in the floor or those that bisect the room should be addressed immediately because they suggest conflict between the occupants.

While marble floors may be suitable for entertainment areas, they are too cold for the bedroom. Warm surfaces such as wooden parquet and tiles are preferred. If you have marble floors in your bedrooms, placing rugs on them will alleviate the material's yin nature.

Column No 59: April 30, 2006

Centre of the Home (In the Clear)

Ideally, the centre of your home – whether it's a passageway or the living room – should be unobstructed, allowing energy to circulate. The orientation and age of an apartment may cause the wealth sector to be located in the middle. If it is enclosed (by a bedroom, for example), the wealth *chi* will be locked, causing the occupants to have financial difficulties.

For those living in regularly shaped, square or rectangular units, identifying the centre is simple. But a lot of apartments in Hong Kong have unorthodox configurations, so feng shui masters will use either house plans or their own experience and judgment to locate the centre.

Several scenarios should be avoided at all costs. Having a kitchen in the centre of the home will result in problems with health and wealth. A toilet in the centre does not augur well for the occupants' health, while a staircase (especially a spiral one) in the centre leads to disputes.

A storeroom at your home's heart will cause stagnancy, with your family feeling lethargic and unmotivated. A home without a central point because of the presence of a lift shaft or service stairs may result in a deterioration in the occupants' interpersonal relationships. If you experience problems in houses or apartments with these designs, seek advice from a feng shui professional.

Column No 68: July 2, 2006

Internal Poison Arrows (Cutting Corners)

Aggressive energy originating from 'poison arrows' can be present indoors as well as outside. When looking out the window of a bedroom or an office, the main threat is likely to come from the edges of an adjacent building that is at an angle to you. The distance between the sharp edge and your office or room should also be considered. If the sharp edge is a significant distance away, its effects will be minimal. Not every adjacent structure is a poison arrow, and each one needs to be assessed on a case-by-case basis.

Indoors, you are at risk from a poison arrow when the edge of a pillar or another desk is aimed directly at you. Keeping one's perspective with regard to poison arrows is important. Just because a pillar is present in an office does not mean that sitting close to it will expose you to *sha chi* - it is how you sit relative to it that matters. When you sit parallel to a pillar or a colleague's desk, there are no poison arrows to contend with.

When one is in the path of poison arrows for prolonged periods of time, there is an increased chance of headaches, irritability and poor concentration. Relocate yourself so that you do not work or sit in the path of one. You may also use blinds, curtains or screens to block the view of the offending structure.

Column No 80: September 24, 2006

Apartment Shapes (Staying in Shape)

It's advisable to live in those apartments or houses that are of a regular shape - square or rectangular - as they allow chi to circulate smoothly throughout the living space. While some people regard irregularly shaped units as aesthetically pleasing, they are not ideal, because in them, chi will travel in a haphazard fashion, leaving occupants feeling unsettled.

Units that are circular are yang in nature and are more suited to commercial activities. L- and U-shaped properties lack a centre and are also not recommended because family conflicts can be a problem for the occupants.

Triangular-shaped units represent the fire element and are therefore excessively yang. Residents will be prone to injuries resulting from mishaps with fire. There's little you can do about the shape of an irregular apartment, so it's best to avoid moving into one.

Of equal, if not more, importance is the shape of the rooms within your home. Even if your unit is rectangular, its benefits are negated if your bedroom or living room is irregular, with several jutting corners. A common solution to the problem is to create a regularly shaped room by adding built-in cabinets. For example, L-shaped rooms can be altered by turning the protruding space into a walk-in closet demarcated by a door or screen.

Column No 81: October 1, 2006

Missing Sectors (Missing Links)

Under one feng shui principle, the living space of a home is divided into nine sectors (eight cardinal and inter-cardinal sectors plus the centre). Family members are then linked to a specific sector. For instance, the father is associated with the northwest sector, the mother with the southwest and the youngest daughter with the west.

Thus, if the northwest sector is 'missing', the head of the household might encounter professional or health problems. However, if the northwest sector has a protrusion that makes it slightly larger than the other sectors, this augurs well for the patriarch's prospects. After applying this principle to modern living, one can understand why feng shui masters recommend residences of a regular shape.

A sector is considered missing when it is less than two-thirds of the other sectors, so do not be overly concerned if there are slight differences in surface area between sectors in your home. One school of thought states that missing sectors may hinder certain aspects of your life (for example, romance or wealth), but this is not a traditional principle.

If you encounter difficulties in an irregularly shaped residence, enlist the help of a professional. Simplistic solutions, such as covering a wall with mirrors to expand the missing sector, may not work.

Column No 82: October 8, 2006

Ceilings (Looking Up)

There shouldn't be any sharp or irregular structures above your head when you are sleeping, sitting, eating or working. Ensure your work desk, chair and bed don't have any lights or fans hanging directly above them. You should move your furniture or remove the feature overhead. Ideally, there should always be a flat ceiling without any protrusions or hollows above you.

For those with sloping or vaulted ceilings, ensure beds and chairs aren't placed below the lowest part of the ceiling. Don't install a false ceiling without professional feng shui advice. When the height of a room is significantly reduced - to around 2 metres - occupants will feel a sense of urgency and pressure, which may result in anxiety and headaches.

When a room or office has an uneven ceiling (perhaps because of air-conditioning ducts) consider using it as a storeroom or guest bedroom.

If you sleep or work in a room with overhead sewerage or water pipes, ensure the bed or desk is not directly underneath them. Alternatively, reduce the pipes' negative effects by covering them.

Column No 90: December 3, 2006

Internal Stairs (Stairways to Heaven)

For those of us who live in multistorey properties, the nature and type of internal staircases should be noted. A standard staircase is preferable to a spiral type for practical purposes, but the latter only poses a significant problem if it is located at the exact centre of the living space, signifying a corkscrew through the heart of the home.

In such a case, occupants will be prone to stress and cardiac problems. It is not advisable to live in properties where there are two prominent staircases or when the main staircase splits into two sections as it approaches another floor. This signifies possible conflict between family members or a couple.

Some feng shui masters feel staircases with open spaces in between the steps will allow chi to leak through, preventing positive energy from reaching the floor above.

The stairs should not be too steep, as the additional effort needed to climb them may translate into obstacles in the occupants' daily lives. The area beneath the stairs should be used only for storage, not for lounging or dining in, or to house an altar, as this area is constantly walked over.

It's best to avoid moving into a unit where the front door opens directly onto stairs that lead to the floor below, as all chi that enters the property will then funnel downstairs.

Column No 92: December 17, 2006

Pillars (Pillar Talk)

Pillars may be an unavoidable feature of a building's design, but they are not positive ones and there are clear feng shui guidelines about their position. For instance, the front entrance to your home or office should not have a pillar directly in front of it. This will block the flow of positive energy towards the property.

Inside your home, there should not be any doors that open directly into a pillar or the sharp energy it exudes will mix with the energy that enters through the door, adversely affecting the overall nature of the room. This applies to both cylindrical and square pillars.

Placing a desk or bed between two pillars is not recommended as it is believed they will exert a 'squeezing effect', resulting in poor concentration or sleep. Sitting parallel to a lone pillar is acceptable. Don't sit at an angle to a square one, though, or its sharp edges will be directed to your side or back, thereby impairing focus and performance.

It is impossible to eliminate structural pillars, so under such conditions, feng shui masters may advise you to relocate your front door or furniture. Screens, plants and fabrics can also be used to cover or camouflage the pillar to reduce its negative effects.

Column No 119: July 8, 2007

Plot Shapes (Get in Shape)

In feng shui terms, free-standing houses are best served by plots that are rectangular, or failing that ones that are narrower at the front, and broader and higher at the rear. Plots with these characteristics suggest the occupants will prosper, with future generations enjoying further good fortune. The opposite effect will be produced by a plot with the opposite attributes: descendants will not enjoy the same benefits that the current occupants have.

Some feng shui masters recommend installing lights on poles to lift the energy of a property. Planting bushes and trees at the front of a house 'turns' one that narrows into one that is square. Relocating the front entrance so the lower end becomes the front end is another option.

For those living in apartments, the overall shape of your flat is important. Avoid moving into apartments that tail off or narrow significantly from the main door to a single room. It's better to choose those with a regular shape.

The plot in which your apartment building stands is another consideration: there should be a higher structure behind it (a building or mountain). If the plot is on the edge of a precipice, occupants will feel extremely unsettled.

Column No 121: July 22, 2007

Internal Changes (Changing Places)

The feng shui of your home may be altered by seemingly innocuous activities. As such, renovations should not be carried out in inappropriate sectors, which are determined by the year.

For instance, you should not knock down a wall in the Grand Duke sector, the area corresponding to the current year's Chinese zodiac animal. If renovations are unavoidable, consult an experienced feng shui professional to find out when would be the best time to do the work.

Although water fountains are used to promote wealth, their placement within your home may have the opposite effect on your fortunes. If you are in a happy relationship and inadvertently encourage the romance sector with a fountain, you may discover a third party complicating your personal situation. Water features should be introduced only after seeking professional advice.

Hanging prints or mirrors without advice may also impair the feng shui of your home. For instance, placing pictures of wild animals with their mouths open and teeth bared directly opposite family photos may adversely affect the health of the people in the photos. In a teenager's room, multiple images of dead celebrities, especially those who have suffered a tragic end, may induce melancholia.

Column No 139: November 26, 2007

Use of Glass (Clear as Glass)

To give narrow areas an illusion of space, interior designers often opt for glass partitions, which maximize light and create a feeling of openness. From a feng shui perspective, this increases the level of yang energy, in turn improving the circulation of *chi*, causing occupants to feel more relaxed and energetic. However, one should be aware of certain feng shui aspects.

Using a frosted-glass partition directly opposite the front door will cause both positive and negative energy to exit your home. Frosted glass reflects indiscriminately; occupants will encounter obstacles and experience lost opportunities, as beneficial *chi* will be unable to enter the home.

Replacing a solid wall in an en-suite bathroom with a glass partition will improve the lighting but make sure the toilet is not visible from the bedroom, otherwise negative energy will circulate, easily, resulting in poor health.

When a glass partitions is used in the kitchen, the stove may be visible from the dining or living room. This could create financial problems as the stove is believed to be where the occupants' wealth is generated and this arrangement will cause favourable energy to dissipate.

Reducing the transparency of the partition should alleviate this problem.

Column No 142: December 16, 2007

Wallpaper (Keep it Simple)

The right choice of wallpaper can make a living space more aesthetically pleasing and give it a renewed sense of vibrancy. However, using complicated and dense designs in a room that is already filled with furniture will result in an excessively yang space. Occupants could find it difficult to concentrate and become irritable.

This is especially true of children's rooms and nurseries, where simple and light designs will make a child feel calm and settled. In contrast, dark colours and sombre designs will cause them to be moody and melancholic. Some children may even be fearful of sleeping in their room, as excessively yin environments will increase their fear of the dark.

In humid regions like Southeast Asia, wallpaper is prone to peeling. Watermarks and stains also become visible. The occupants of a home with such wallpaper will be prone to arthritis, lethargy and breathing problems. Should this occur, replace the wallpaper immediately.

Ceilings should also not be covered with peeling wallpaper otherwise occupants may find themselves feeling disoriented and susceptible to dizzy spells.

Column No 143: December 23, 2007

Irregular Rooms (Outside the Box)

According to traditional feng shui principles, a room or office should be square or rectangular in shape, as this will allow chi to circulate evenly throughout. Rooms with irregular or sharp corners will have negative energy accumulating in the irregular areas, causing occupants to feel unsettled. For instance, your bedroom or living room may be mostly rectangular but a triangular section, associated with fire, attached to the end would be extremely yang in nature.

To rectify this, demarcate the rest of the room from the irregular sector by using a solid wooden screen, bookshelf or cabinet. You may also install thick, indoor curtains to symbolically shield off the problematic sector. For living rooms, a row of plotted plants is another solution. The irregular sector can then be used for storage. Depending on its size, you may be able to use cabinets or doors to cover this space.

Using an irregular area of a room for study or relaxation is not advisable as you will be prone to headaches, insomnia, accidents and heart and blood-pressure problems.

As the issue is structural, covering the walls of a protruding sector with mirrors (so as to make it 'disappear') will not be effective, nor will painting it a different colour from the rest of the room.

Column No 160: May 4, 2008

Feng Shui and Interior Design (Chic or Chi?)

There are some interior designers who may be familiar with basic feng shui principles, but the majority of feng shui masters are not acquainted with the doctrines behind interior design, which may lead to some discord if you hire one of each to help you lay out your home.

There are also situations in which interior design and feng shui principles are in opposition; for instance, having a front door that faces a large window or balcony may allow you to maximise light and enjoy views when entering a home but *chi* or energy that enters the living space will be immediately funneled out, preventing positive energy (i.e. wealth energy) from accumulating.

Then there are feng shui consultants who insist clients display Chinese statues and paintings, which may clash with an otherwise Western design theme.

It's up to you how much store you put in advice offered by both parties, but feng shui masters should preferably be contacted before the initial design work is carried out, so the sectors of a home that suit each family member can be identified.

Once the designs have been completed, the master can then be consulted again to see whether any feng shui violations can be rectified before construction and renovation is carried out.

Column No 232: October 4, 2009

Chapter 12

Mirrors

Mirrors in the Bedroom

Being able to see yourself reflected in the mirror when lying in bed is considered bad feng shui. According to the traditional Chinese explanation, our souls leave our bodies when we sleep and return when we wake up. Having a mirror reflecting our body causes confusion for the soul, which doesn't know which body it should return to. This results in the occupant being tired despite long hours of sleep.

Regardless of the validity of this explanation, having a mirror reflecting the bed will result in poor sleep and arguments between the occupants of the room. Having mirrors on cupboards that reflect the bed sideways on is also unacceptable.

When it comes to mirrors in the bedroom, they should ideally be located inside the wardrobe or in a separate dressing room. When there is a dresser in the room, ensure that its mirror is angled away from the bed - you should not be able to see your reflection when lying down.

Should the mirror opposite the bed be fixed to the wall or a door, try covering it up with paper or curtains. You should notice the difference to your sleep.

And finally, while mirrors on the ceiling may have some appeal, they will not help improve your sleep as they combine two drawbacks: that of a mirror and that of something overhanging the bed.

Column No 7: April 17, 2005

Mirrors Inside Your Home (On Reflection)

Mirrors are one of the most controversial tools in feng shui. Some masters employ them to reflect attacking energy, while others insist their use is overrated. However, it is universally accepted mirrors should never be placed inside and directly opposite the front door as positive and negative energies will be reflected back when it is opened. This will lead to obstacles in professional and personal life.

Mirrors placed opposite windows can attract energy from outside. Picturesque mountains and clear water outside windows are ideal, but in Hong Kong there is a greater chance of seeing neighbouring buildings, some of which may be in need of renovation or be under construction.

Do not hang a mirror in your home without taking into account what it reflects. Mirrors should not reflect the occupants when they are asleep in the bedroom and should be hung with discretion in the dining room.

Some people like to hang small round mirrors on the inside of windows to fend off sharp corners of buildings. This is not recommended - drawing the curtains or blinds is more effective. Such placement is usually unwarranted because the structures are relatively innocuous. Poor placement can cause more harm than good. If in doubt, seek the opinion of a feng shui consultant.

Column No 19: July 10, 2005

Ba Gua Mirrors (Mirror, Mirror on the Wall)

In Southeast Asia, it is not uncommon to see *ba gua* mirrors hanging above apartment doors. These mirrors are used to deflect attacking, or negative, energy and should be used only outside the home.

Ba Gua refers to the collection of eight trigrams (line formations derived from the *I Ching* or *Book of Changes*) that reflect the yin and yang energies in the universe. On *ba gua* Mirrors, the trigrams are arranged in the Former Heaven Sequence, with Heaven (three unbroken lines) at the top and Earth (three broken lines) at the bottom. This is the correct way to hang a mirror. If it is hung the opposite way, it could attract unwanted yin, or spectral energy.

Ba gua mirrors can also be convex or concave. Convex mirrors are able to deflect attacking energy from structures such as sharp edges or pillars. Although concave mirrors are also able to deflect energy negative energy, they can also concentrate the energy and redirect it back, thereby injuring others. Cases have arisen where neighbours have noticed a convex *ba gua* mirror opposite their front door and unwittingly retaliated by hanging a concave *ba gua* mirror.

Outside Asia, some feng shui consultants prefer to use plain mirrors due to concerns regarding cultural and religious sensitivities.

Column No 24: August 14, 2005

Mirrors (Mirror Image)

In traditional feng shui, mirrors don't open up spaces in rooms or replace missing elements. They reflect back what is captured in them – whether it's good or bad. Mirrors can't choose the type of energy they reflect. That's why having one on the wall directly opposite your front door will result in missed opportunities - as favourable and unfavourable energy is deflected. A small *ba gua* mirror placed above your front door, on the other hand, will deflect attacking energy from passageways and sharp corners.

In living and dining rooms, mirrors can be used to increase the yang energy as long as family members don't sit with their backs to them for long periods. The view the mirror reflects should be positive as it's better to have beautiful mountains and harbour views reflected into your home rather than old buildings or your neighbour's home.

Some masters recommend placing mirrors behind stoves that stand directly opposite an entrance so the cook can see who enters. Full-length mirrors that reflect the whole stove, though, will cause instability in the food.

Dressing-table mirrors should never reflect the bed as this may affect marital relations. If possible, place a mirror on the same wall as the headboard. Alternatively, hang one on the inside of a wardrobe.

Column No 70: July 16, 2006

Dresser (Man in the Mirror)

The dressing or vanity table plays a vital role in feng shui in the bedroom because the attached mirror can disrupt the sleep of the room's occupant. A dressing table should never be placed at the foot of the bed because the mirror will reflect back onto the occupant while they sleep.

It is believed the soul exits the body when we sleep. Having a mirror reflecting image during the night means the soul becomes confused about which body to enter upon waking, resulting in lethargy and restlessness, even after a long night's sleep.

Similar disruption occurs when the mirror is at the side of the bed, reflecting its occupants' image from there. This may lead to more conflict in a relationship. Placing the mirror so it looks out well above, but still across, the bed does not solve the problem. The best solution is to relocate the dressing table.

This piece of furniture should not be situated opposite the entrance to the bedroom as this will reflect positive chi from your room. Nor should the mirror face the en suite bathroom, as this may allow negative chi form the bathroom and toilet to infiltrate your sleeping area. Also, if the dresser faces another mirror, this may magnify unsettling energy, causing poor sleep.

Column No 116: June 17, 2007

204

Mirrors in Interior Design (Mirror Effect)

Interior designers use mirrors to increase the sense of depth, light and space in a home. However, if placed carelessly, they may cause more harm than good.

While full-length mirrors can be placed in the entrance hall of an apartment, make sure they are not directly opposite the front door, so you don't see your reflection when you enter the house. They should not be on the wall that is immediately diagonal to the front door. Positive energy, including wealth energy, could be reflected away from your home. Mirrors should not be directly opposite the doorways to rooms such as the bedroom or study.

You should also be aware of the positioning of large mirrors in the dining room. Try to ensure that you do not sit with your back to a mirror or have just parts of your body reflected in a mirror when dining. This may cause arguments at mealtimes.

Filling an entire wall with a mirror to fill in a 'missing sector' is also ineffective. This virtual approach may cause problems because being reflected in a large mirror for any length of time will make a person feel uncomfortable.

Column No 183: October 12, 2008

Chapter 13

The Office and Work

The Office

In Hong Kong we spend most, if not all, of our working day in an office, so it is important to spare a thought for our surroundings. The right office feng shui can ward off sniping colleagues, relieve tension and promote productivity, but get it wrong and there will be trouble.

Perhaps the most important aspect of office feng shui is the position we sit in while working. If possible, try to ensure your back is to a wall or partition. Sitting with your back to a door or window leave you vulnerable to attack from backstabbing rivals. Concentration and performance will be affected if you have a passageway, stairs, water cooler or main entrance behind you.

And, while a breathtaking view might seem desirable, there is a danger of becoming accustomed to it and, in time, finding it a distraction rather than an inspiration. For those fortunate enough to have their own office, sit facing the door so everyone who enters or walks past can be seen. If your back is to a window, keep the curtains drawn.

The layout of an office can create good or bad feng shui. Try placing partitions between desks so employees have their own work space or cubicle, which will give them a sense of security and privacy, and ultimately lead to efficiency and harmony in the workplace.

Column No 1: March 6, 2005

Business Cards (Card Sharp)

In Hong Kong, exchanging business cards occurs at every meeting. A business card serves as a source of contact information and a vital first impression; thus its design and colour should not be taken for granted. Feng Shui guidelines need to be followed when choosing card colours.

Careers and occupations are assigned to one of the natural five elements: water, wood, fire, earth and metal. For instance, those working in media and public relations are involved in communications, which is represented by water. Law and finance are metal careers, because the former involves a degree of power and the latter deals with currency, traditionally metal coins.

There are also specific colours associated with each element. Fire is represented by red, orange, pink, purple, magenta and vermillion. Earth colours include yellow, beige and shades of brown.

After identifying the element associated with your career, choose a colour that supports it. Consult the cycle of the elements; for example, water sustains wood. When it comes to colours to avoid, the cycle of destruction should be noted; wood is destroyed by metal that chops it down. Thus, if you are in a wood career, your card should have water colours and not metal colours.

Column No 29: September 18, 2005

Water Careers (Water Colours)

Water occupations can be divided into three main groups. The first includes jobs involving actual water such as naval service, fishing, beverage production and laundering. Because water is a fluid element, the second group includes jobs associated with movement: professions concerned with shipping, transport and travel, for instance. Traditionally, water has connotations of intelligence and communications, so the third group encompasses the media, journalism, private investigation and music.

If you are in a water profession, the colours of your business card should support the element. Thus, your card should contain colours that represent water or metal, because metal liquefies to produce 'water'. Water colours include black, navy and light blue, while metal colours include grey, silver, white and gold.

The colours to avoid are those of earth, wood and fire. In the cycle of destruction, earth overwhelms water, so yellow, brown and beige are not recommended. Water feeds wood, so green is best avoided and, while water douses fire and is used to control it, it suggests conflict, so red, orange, pink, purple and magenta are also inadvisable.

Using the wrong colour may be detrimental to your career.

Column No 30: September 25, 2005

Wood Careers (Wood Work)

There are three main groups of wood careers, the first type being those that are directly associated with wood and its products: jobs involving furniture and textiles, vegetarian restaurateurs, florists, fruit and vegetable vendors, perfumers, botanists and herbalists.

Paper is derived from wood and accounts for the second main group of wood careers: paper/stationery makers and suppliers, publishers, administrators, writers, artists and other creative types.

Traditionally, the qualities associated with wood are caring for and nurturing others, which leads to the third group of wood careers: social work, counsellors, teachers, religious leaders, pharmacists and other medical occupations.

In the cycle of birth, water nourishes wood. Thus, those in wood careers should have business cards in colours associated with water (black, navy and light blue) or wood (green). Colours to avoid include those of the metal element (white, grey, silver, gold) because metal is used to chop down wood. Fire colours (red, orange, purple, pink) are also not recommended.

Don't panic if your doctor's card has a white background as this is usually combined with black lettering.

Column No 31: October 2, 2005

Fire Careers (Bright Sparks)

Fire careers can be divided into three groups, the first being technical jobs in which fire plays a major part: those concerned with manufacturing explosives, chemicals and flammable substances, electronics, lighting, repairs, assembly and refining.

The next group of fire careers covers the service industry: jobs associated with cooking and spas that offer saunas and hot springs. Finally, fire is also linked with occupations that emphasise appearance and expression: those in beauty parlours, advertising, design, interior decoration, photography and performance (acting, entertainment), and jobs that involve public speaking.

In the cycle of birth, fire is kindled by wood. Those involved in fire careers should have business cards with appropriate colours: red, orange, pink or purple for fire; or green for wood. Water colours (black and all shades of blue) should be avoided, as should those that represent the earth (yellow, shades of brown, beige and cream).

Metal colours (white, gold, silver, grey) are also not recommended because fire melts metal, suggesting conflict.

With these principles in mind, it becomes obvious why the predominant colour scheme in traditional Chinese restaurants is red (which is also linked to prosperity).

Column No 32: October 9, 2005

Earth Careers (Dirty Work)

Earth careers are divided into two main groups: those associated with earth, such as the building industry, mining, property development and sale, and feng shui; and those associated with agriculture and products derived from the earth, such as farming, plastics and ceramics, and the working of gems and stones. As earth is associated with trust, being a consultant others rely on is also considered an earth profession.

In the cycle of birth, fire produces ash and therefore earth. The appropriate colours for business cards for people in earth industries are those connected to fire (red, orange, purple and magenta) and earth (yellow, beige, cream and shades of brown). Unsuitable colours include green, which relates to wood (which attacks earth) and black and blue, which signify water (which is in conflict with earth).

White, silver, grey and gold, colours that represent metal, are also not suited as metal is derived from earth and drains it.

Feng Shui consultants, therefore, have predominantly red or beige/cream cards. Consultants' business cards should not only support earth but also the industry that they are associated with. Educational consultants, for example, should have colours representing wood (green) or water (black, blue) together with red, denoting a consultancy.

Column No 33: October 16, 2005

Metal Careers (Steel Yourself)

Metal careers are divided into three main groups, with the first of those directly associated with metal. These careers include engineering and the manufacturing and marketing of metal products: tools and cutting instruments, cutlery, electrical appliances, computers, automobiles, spare parts and arms.

Traditionally, metal is associated with justice and power, which accounts for the second group of metal careers: those in the legal profession, law enforcement and security, martial arts and human resources. Because early Chinese currency was made from metal, the third group of metal careers involves banking and finance.

Earth produces metal in the birth cycle of elements, so suitable colours for business cards for those working in metal occupations are white, silver, grey or gold (symbolizing metal) and brown, beige, cream or yellow (representing earth).

Inappropriate colours include red, orange, purple or pink (fire melts metal), as well as blue or black (water drains metal, thereby weakening it). Using green on business cards is also not recommended, as metal attacks wood, which suggests success will be achieved only through conflict.

With this in mind, it's obvious why bankers should have business cards with a white, beige or cream background.

Column No 34: October 23, 2005

Office/Shop Entrances (State of Emergency)

Feng Shui principles apply to commercial properties as well as to residential ones. In an office or shop, for instance, no emergency apparatus - such as fire extinguishers, axes or hoses – should be directly opposite the entrance, otherwise occupants will experience obstacles in their careers. Such items should be immediately relocated. The hooks and screws used to fasten them to the walls should also be removed and any holes or cavities left in the area should also be filled in.

Also, the entrance to your office should also not be facing the toilets, as this may adversely affect the health of staff members. Nor should there be any lifts, fire staircases, electrical fuse boxes or power rooms directly opposite the office entrance, as positive chi will be carried away in the first two instances and unsettling energy will enter in the latter two. Having a square or round pillar in front of your office door signifies difficulties for your business or work. In these instances, relocate your entrance or consider moving.

It is preferable not to move into commercial properties with entrances that directly face those of other units, as this may result in disputes. If this is unavoidable, ensure your entrance is not smaller than your neighbour's or more positive energy will enter his unit than yours.

Column No 124: August 12, 2007

Reception Area (A Warm Welcome)

When entering an office, our first impressions are gained from the reception area, which is why the location of the receptionist's desk is important. If the desk is aligned with the main entrance, the door will open towards the receptionist, placing the company in a vulnerable position. Also vulnerable is the receptionist who sits with their back to the main entrance, resulting in visitors surprising them with their presence. The reception desk should also not be placed at such an angle to the entrance that the poison arrows from its corners hit the main door.

Nor should the receptionist sit directly facing the main entrance, otherwise there may be an increased instance of staff turnover. Ideally, the receptionist should be out of the direct path of an opening main door, yet facing it. If space constraints dictate that the receptionist has no choice but to face the entrance directly, use a desk that has a counter at the front; this will provide protection from incoming chi.

To prevent the receptionist being distracted, a table should be set between their desk and the pathway taken by people passing through the area.

The desk should not be placed directly in front of a pillar, as this might limit the space the receptionist has to move around in, which not only results in discomfort but also decreased productivity.

Column No 125: August 19, 2007

Windows in Offices (Working Miracles)

Modern offices tend to have a window on one or more sides. Regardless of how attractive the view is, it is not recommended for you to sit facing a window, as this may result in distraction and a decreasing appreciation of the view. If you sit with your back to the entrance, you will be vulnerable to rumours and backstabbing from your associates.

It is preferable to sit with your side to the view and face the door, so that you are able to glance out of the window from time to time. If you have no choice but to sit facing a window, try to minimise the glare by keeping the curtains partly drawn. You can also arrange furniture or plants to partly obscure the view.

If there are windows on multiple walls, ensure the window that lies behind you when you are working becomes a virtual wall by keeping the curtains closed.

Should there be pillars within your office, ensure you do not sit with your back to the edge of one. Nor should a pillar interfere with your path when leaving your desk. For instance, if a pillar is adjacent to your desk and means you have to squeeze out whenever you leave, you may encounter obstacles in your work that will result in decreased productivity. Relocate your desk or reduce its dimensions so you have ample space to move around.

Column No 127: September 2, 2007

Meetings (In the Hot Seat)

When attending a business meeting, it is preferable to sit with your back to the wall, facing the entrance. Regardless of whether you are the host or a guest, you should not sit with your back to the door, or near it. When this is not possible, adhere to the following guidelines.

Seats that are parallel to the entrance are acceptable if they allow you to see who is entering the room. Sitting with your back to the window leaves you vulnerable unless there is some barrier behind you, such as drawn curtains. Alternatively, position in front of the solid wall between windows. You should also avoid sitting in the seat nearest the toilets.

Meanwhile, you should take note of the ceiling above your seat. Do not sit under beams or protrusions such as fans, air-conditioning units or lights. Do not sit directly at the corners of the table as this will cut positive energy directed toward you.

Some feng shui masters even advocate taking a compass to meetings so you can 'tap into' your favourable directions. However, negative effects exerted by visible structures will nullify the benefits of directions. With these principles in mind, it is preferable to be early for important meetings so you can grab the most fortuitous seat.

Column No 128: September 9, 2007

Glass Walls (Divided We Fall)

Those fortunate enough to have their own office may have a glass wall on one or more sides. While glass partitions let light in and create a sense of space, they may also increase the vulnerability of those working behind them as they are always visible to their colleagues. Those in positions of seniority may find their authority questioned.

Glass walls should not have any horizontal or vertical lines cutting across the walls. Such adornments can make a person appear to be split in half, which does not augur well for his employment within the company.

Glass panels that have a cross on them make the person in that office a potential scapegoat for company problems. An 'X' symbol represents the fire element; having such a design on a partition results in disputes.

To reduce the negative effects of glass partitions, consider using vertical blinds, which confer privacy and protection. Do not draw the blinds fully as this may give your colleagues the impression you are isolating yourself. Instead, pull them to half-way so you still appear approachable.

Alternatively, you may use plants or furniture to form a protective barrier. Darkening the glass or using a one-way partition are not recommended as they suggest secrecy, which will not build trust with your colleagues.

Column 129: September 16, 2007

Departments (Pole Position)

Allocating departments to their appropriate sector within an office will ensure a company runs smoothly. The managing director should be in the power position, which is generally the area diagonally opposite the main entrance. It is preferable for him/her to be in a separate room, otherwise their ability to delegate and manage may be compromised.

The sales and marketing department should be situated close to the entrance. As there is considerable activity and interaction between members of this department, an open-plan arrangement is acceptable. The accounts and human resources department should be away from the entrance and not easily visible to visitors. Ensure they are not adjacent to toilets, otherwise the wealth of the company might be flushed away.

Feng shui masters who practice the Flying Stars method locate departments according to the orientation and age of a property. Departments with considerable activity, such as sales, are placed in yang areas, where there are positive water stars, which stimulate wealth. The managing director and the human resources departments are placed in yin sectors, where there are calming mountain stars, which help them focus.

Column No 131: September 30, 2007

Company Logos (In Good Company)

Regardless of the nature of an enterprise or shop, a company logo is vital as gives an all-important first impression to potential customers. A company's logo should be prominently displayed so those entering its office see it instantly. For example, it can be centred above the receptionist and lit up. It should not be on the base of the receptionist's desk, as this is foot level, implying the company will be kicked around. It should also not be placed on the left (male) or right (female) of centre, or one sex will dominate the company.

Businesses can be divided into groups corresponding to the five elements: wood, fire, earth, metal and water. For instance, property firms are associated with the earth while manufacturing involving the use of chemicals is linked with fire.

Ideally, the colours of a logo should reflect the nature of the company concerned. For example, water-related enterprises should include black or blue in their logos. The shape of a logo is also important, so businesses associated with wood should have symbols that are rectangular and vertical.

Cycles of production and destruction should also be taken into account. For instance, wood feeds fire. Hence, it would be acceptable for fire-related businesses to use shades of green and rectangular shapes in their logos.

However, wood, as a tree, grows into and depletes the earth. So if a property company has green rectangles in its logo, its earning potential would be compromised.

Column No 132: October 7, 2007

221

Wood Companies (Wood Work)

Enterprises associated with wood can be divided into three main groups. The first involves products derived from wood or plants, such as florists, herbalists, furniture production and fruit and vegetable trading. The second is associated with paper, which is derived from wood. This group includes publishers, printers and bookshops. The wood element is associated with nurturing and concern for others, so includes schools and universities, charities and pharmaceutical and healthcare companies.

The favourable elements for such businesses are wood and the element that produces it (water). Varying shades of green and blue should therefore be used in the logos of wood-related companies. Wood is associated with tall, thin and narrow shapes such as the rectangle; water is represented by wavy, irregular designs.

Colours to avoid include those representing metal (white, grey, gold, silver) as well as those symbolising fire (red, orange, purple and pink). Shapes to avoid for logos are circles and ovals (which reflect metal) and triangles (which are of the fire element).

As earth is overwhelmed by the wood element, its colours (yellow, beige, shades of brown) and its shape (square) are not recommended either, as earth can ultimately drain the energy of wood.

Column No 133: October 14, 2007

Fire Companies (Playing With Fire)

Companies associated with the fire element fall into three main groups. The first includes enterprises such as electricity supply, lighting and oil and gas exploration, all of which use fire in their production.

Parts of the service industry are in the second group of fire enterprises and these include restaurants and spas. Fire can be used to express yourself, which accounts for the third group of fire companies: event organisation and photography.

Fire requires wood to kindle. Hence, colours that can be used in the logos of fire-related companies include those that represent fire and those that represent wood (shades of green). Favourable shapes include triangles (symbolising fire) and rectangles (representing wood).

In the cycle of destruction, fire is destroyed by water. Thus, the colours black and blue and wavy, irregular patterns are not recommended for logos of fire-related enterprises. Since fire burns and depletes earth's energy, yellow, brown and other earth tones and squares are also not recommended.

While metal is destroyed by fire, it ultimately exhausts it, so it is not advisable to use the colours white, silver and grey or circular and oval shapes in the company logo.

Column No 134: October 21, 2007

Earth Companies (Back To Earth)

There are two main groups of companies associated with the earth element. The first involves construction, mining and real estate, including development and sales. The second encompasses enterprises involved with the products that are derived from the earth: jewellery, ceramics, agriculture and farming. Trust is represented by the earth element, which is why consulting is considered an earth enterprise.

In the productive cycle, earth is formed by fire. Thus, appropriate colours for earth-related company logos include those that symbolise earth (yellow, beige, brown and other earth tones) or fire (red, orange, pink and purple). Shapes that can be incorporated into the logos of such companies include squares and triangles, which represent the earth and fire elements respectively.

In the cycle of destruction, wood destroys earth. Hence, rectangles and shades of green should not be used in the logos of earth-related companies. Even though earth soaks up water, it ultimately drains away. Therefore, the use of water related colours (black and blue) or shapes (wavy, irregular patterns) are not recommended.

Earth produces metal, thereby reducing its energy. This makes it unwise to use white, grey and silver for the logos of earth companies. Circles and ovals should be avoided as well.

Column No 135: October 28, 2007

Metal Companies (Test Your Metal)

There are three main groups of metal-related enterprises. The first group consists of those directly related to products made from metal such as vehicles, machinery, tools, utensils and equipment.

Metal is associated with power and justice, which explains why security and law firms are considered metal-type companies. Because of metal coins, banks, finance and accounting companies compose the final group.

In the cycle of birth, metal is derived from earth. Hence, besides colours associated with metal (white, grey and silver), earth colours (yellow, beige and brown) can be used in the logos of metal-related companies. Shapes that can be used include circles and ovals, which represent metal, and squares, which symbolise earth.

Metal is destroyed by fire, so it is not advisable to use triangles or colours associated with fire. Metal melts to form water, thereby draining its essence. Thus, the colours and shapes associated with water are not recommended in the logos of metal-type companies. Metal cuts down wood so the use of green and rectangles should be avoided too.

With these principles in mind, you can understand why grey or silver are the colours of choice for the logos of many banks and finance firms.

Column No 136: November 5, 2007

Water Companies (Test the Water)

Water-related companies can be broken down into three main groups. The first consists of companies in which water is directly involved, such as laundromats and drinks companies.

The second group encompasses those associated with movement, such as shipping firms, travel agencies and relocation companies. The water element represents communication and intelligence, so public relation companies, marketing firms and media outlets make up the final group of water companies.

In the cycle of birth, water is produced by metal. Hence, when designing the logo of water companies, colours representing water (black or blue) and metal (white, silver and grey) can be used. Wavy patterns, and oval and circles are suitable. Water is destroyed by earth, so it is not advisable to use yellow, beige or brown or squares in a water-related company's logo.

Wood is produced by water, so its energy and essence is reduced. Therefore, green and rectangular shapes should not be used. Although water overwhelms fire, it is ultimately exhausted by it. Using fire-related colours (red, orange, purple and pink) and triangles in the logo may result in success achieved only through considerable effort.

Column No 137: November 12, 2007

What Lies Above

For those of us with limited storage space in our homes and offices, it is tempting to place open shelves or glass cabinets on the walls above where we sleep or work. This is not conducive, however, from a feng shui perspective as having objects hanging above your head when you are working or sleeping will result in an increased incidence of headaches.

If you place photos, travel souvenirs or even plaques and awards above your head at your work station, the energy of these objects will press down, making it hard to concentrate and possibly giving you a throbbing headache.

Similarly, if you have shelves at the head of your bed with objects displayed on them, you may discover that you are still tired or have a headache when you wake up. You may also suffer from aches and pains in your neck and shoulders.

Overhanging shelves should preferably be removed but if they are fixed, ensure that they are empty. If the protruding overhead shelves are made of glass or metal, you may cover them with a thick fabric, so that it appears as if there is a drape hanging down.

Column No 223: August 2, 2009

How You Work (Work Wonders)

If you work in an office that has spectacular views do not be tempted to position your desk so that you are facing the vista at all times. There are several reasons for this: first, you will be looking into activity, which is considered yang in nature. This will prevent you from concentrating fully on your work.

In addition, you may also become desensitized to the view, with the consequence that it becomes 'wallpaper'. Finally, the sunlight that filters through will impair your concentration, especially if it is from the setting sun, as that is of a yin quality, being light that belongs to the end of the day.

Neither should your desk be placed directly against a wall. The Ming Tang or Bright Hall formation - the principle that there should always be some space ahead of you that will allow positive energy to accumulate - will not be able to work its magic. Facing a wall at work means that you may encounter setbacks, obstacles and frustration.

Ideally, you should face an open space that does not look directly at a door or window so the Bright Hall formation is simulated. It is preferable to position your desk so any view is to your side and you can look up when taking a break to fully appreciate it.

Column No 224: August 9, 2009

Chapter 14

Other Rooms

The Bathroom

In feng shui, the bathroom and toilet are considered 'wet areas' that will adversely affect the occupants' health if located in unfavourable places. Traditional Chinese houses built according to feng shui principles had the wet areas outside the main living areas. In modern living, we are accustomed to the bathroom being within our living space for convenience and privacy. Does this mean that en suite bathrooms are examples of bad feng shui?

The answer is no. The effects of the bathroom can be determined from its position relative to the main structures in our home, such as the front door, bed and stove. When the bathroom is directly opposite the main entrance or the stove, one will be prone to frequent illnesses. In the bedroom, the part of the body directly opposite the bathroom door when one is sleeping will be affected.

The feng shui problems described above can be solved by installing a solid screen or curtains (should there be space constraints) between the bathroom and the affected structure (e.g. the bed). Alternatively, one can keep the bathroom door closed at all times, but this is less effective and may affect ventilation in your bathroom. The location of the bathroom can also affect one's wealth.

Column No 2: March 13, 2005

Dining Room

The dining room is the sector of the home where occupants gather for meals and catch up on the day's developments. It is considered a personal and intimate space for family and friends to enjoy, which is why some feng shui masters feel that it should not be directly visible from the front door.

With regard to the dining room's layout, it should not be on a lower split level than the living room, as this will result in an accumulation of passive yin energy. The toilet door should also not be immediately visible from the dining room, as the negative energy from this will affect the occupants' health.

While some practitioners feel a mirror placed in the dining room will symbolically double the food being served, please be aware of what the mirror actually reflects, i.e. it should not bring in negative energy from building sites or busy streets. The mirror should also not appear to cut occupants' heads off.

Sitting with your back to a mirror when you are eating will also give you a sense of insecurity and uncertainty. The size of the dining table should also be proportional to the number of family members.

Rectangular or square tables are conducive to dinner conversations and entertaining because people will tend to linger and dine at a leisurely pace. With round tables, food will be eaten quickly with a minimum of fuss and discussion.

Column No 6: April 10, 2005

The Kitchen (What's Cooking?)

The significance of feng shui in the kitchen should never be underestimated. After all, this is where we prepare food, which affects our health and well-being. The most important structure in the kitchen is the stove, considered by some feng shui masters to be an area where wealth is also generated. Hence, it should not be easily visible from one's front door; otherwise wealth might be drained away.

Those with 'exposed' stoves can rectify the situation by placing a barrier such as a screen between the stove and the front door. The kitchen door should also be kept closed.

Another major feng shui problem is caused by stoves (a fire element) being placed directly opposite sinks (a water element). The clash will result in disagreements between a husband and wife. Placing a wooden or green mat between the two fixtures will rectify the situation, but ideally conflict should be avoided. Structures representing water (refrigerators) and fire (ovens, microwave) should also not be located adjacent to each other, or one's health may be adversely affected.

Finally, the toilet and kitchen must be kept as separate as possible. The toilet door should not open opposite the stove, which also shouldn't share the same wall as a toilet. When these situations arise, the stove should be relocated.

Column No 10: May 8, 2005

The Living Room (Inviting Space)

The living room is usually the focal point of any home: the front door often opens onto it and it is the main gathering area. It should be well lit and have more yang than yin energy. The curtains should be left to allow in light and it should not be on a lower level than the rest of the home, as this will result in an accumulation of yin energy. Guests will not find an excessively yin living room inviting.

Chairs in the living area should have good back support and be arranged in a manner conducive to conversation. You should sit with your back to a wall and not to the main door. Consider relocating the television socket if it is on the wall opposite the front door.

There should not be any overhanging beams in the living area but if there are, do not place any chairs or sofas under them. Sitting under these structures for long periods will give you headaches.

Do not have an excess of furniture impeding access into your home from the front door. If your front door cannot open fully because it is blocked by furniture, you may find opportunities that were previously certain fall through at the last minute.

Keep the space near the front door clear at all times to allow chi to circulate. Remember, your living room provides visitors with their first impression, and is usually where chi energy enters the house.

Column No 21: July 24, 2005

The Stove (Cooking with Confidence)

In traditional feng shui, the stove is the third most important object belonging to a house, after the front door and the bed. The stove represents a family's ability to generate wealth and health, so it should lie in a protected position within the kitchen.

It should not be directly opposite the kitchen door; otherwise incoming energy will clash with the stove and adversely affect health and wealth. There should also be no beam pressing down on the stove as this will affect the quality of the food being prepared.

The back of the stove should also be well supported; there should be a solid wall behind it, not an open window, passageway or mirrors. Corners should be avoided when positioning the stove, even if a feng shui consultant has advised it should face the best direction. Having the back angled across a corner denotes instability, a situation that is not redressed by tapping any favourable direction.

Ideally, the person who is preparing food should be able to see anyone who is entering the kitchen. Cooking with your back to the door gives a feeling of insecurity and may affect confidence and earning capacity.

Finally, you should always ensure your stove is clean and fully functional.

Column No 36: November 6, 2005

Kitchen Utensils (Kitchen Sync)

In traditional Chinese kitchens, the stove should not have any knives or other cooking utensils hanging over it. In classical feng shui, the stove is associated with the ability of the home's residents to generate wealth.

When knife blades point at the stove from above, the occupants will run into obstacles in their professional lives that may compromise their earning capacity. Keep the area above the stove clear.

It is inadvisable to eat or drink from bowls, plates, glasses, mugs or cups if they are chipped. Some feng shui masters feel using damaged dishes or vessels will adversely affect one's health, leading to conditions such as heartburn and indigestion. Eating from crockery that is cracked also implies declining financial fortunes.

Chopsticks should always be matching. Some feng shui masters say using mismatched chopsticks may lead to a complicated love life. Also, chopsticks should never be stuck apart vertically into a bowl of rice. This evokes two joss sticks protruding from an urn at worship and is also how chopsticks are placed when food offerings are made to ancestors.

Replicating this yin pattern (associated with praying and the spiritual world) in a yang situation (when dining with others) is offensive as it may be interpreted as beckoning yin energies.

Column 78: September 10, 2006

Storage Areas (Out of Sight)

In developed cities such as Hong Kong, living spaces tend to be small, leaving limited options for storing items not used every day, such as winter clothes, Christmas decorations and sports equipment. For people who have the luxury of a storeroom in their home, some feng shui principles should be followed.

Ideally, a storeroom should not be located opposite the main entrance or be at the centre of the home, as this may lead to the accumulation of stagnant energy. A storeroom should not be so full the door can't be closed and it should be aired and cleared regularly.

While some people may have more difficulty than others in letting go of personal items, it's essential to ask ourselves whether these items are still relevant to our lives and if they could be more useful to others. Keeping electrical appliances that no longer work and cannot be fixed, for instance, serves little purpose.

Remember that areas behind doors (including the main door) should not be used for storage. Doors that are unable to open fully suggest obstacles for the home's occupants, so think twice before placing your vacuum cleaner or tennis racquet behind your bedroom door.

Column 83: October 15, 2006

Toilet Doors and Lids (Flip your Lid)

Some feng shui consultants advocate that toilet doors should always be closed and toilet seats and lids kept down at all times. There are several rationales behind this, one of them being that this will prevent one's wealth being flushed away. Unfortunately, this feng shui 'intervention' has also created much unnecessary tension within families when not everyone subscribes to the theory.

While there is no basis for the toilet seat and lid to be kept down at all times in traditional feng shui teachings, keeping the toilet door closed in certain instances is recommended, but from a health, not wealth, perspective. When the toilet door is opposite or in close proximity to the front door, is clearly visible from the living or dining rooms or is adjacent to the kitchen, keeping the toilet door closed will limit the negative *chi* in the toilet from mixing with the energy already present in the home.

For those who are concerned about poor ventilation, you may keep the toilet door slightly ajar (but not half open) or install a humidifier.

En suites are not considered feng shui problems if the toilet door does not open directly onto any portion of the bed. When it does, keep the toilet door closed when you are asleep.

Column No 85: October 29, 2006

Toilet Location (Smallest Room in the House)

While traditional Chinese homes had 'wet areas' - bathrooms and toilets outside the living space - this type of design is considered unsuitable for modern living. Although bathrooms and toilets are undoubtedly areas where illness energy can accumulate, you shouldn't be so concerned about their negative effects that you allow only one cramped 'wet area' in the home.

When assessing the overall issue, one should focus on a toilet's location, not size. It is not recommended to move into a residence with a lavatory in its centre, adjoining the kitchen or near the stove. Occupants of such homes will be prone to health problems. Unfortunately, there isn't much a feng shui master can do to help because the violations are structural.

While it's unacceptable for the stove to have a flushing toilet directly behind it (separated only by a wall), shifting either the stove or WC will address the issue.

There is a common misconception that having toilets in various sectors of one's home (for example, the southwest) will adversely affect a certain aspect of one's life (such as romance). There is no basis for this in classical feng shui texts, so don't blame the loo for any upheavals in your love life.

Column No 87: November 12, 2006

Kitchen Location (Kitchen Sinkers)

When assessing a property prior to renting or purchasing it, you should take note of the location and layout of the kitchen. For instance, the kitchen should never be in the centre of a home because this equates to the stove burning up the dwelling's heart, resulting in health problems for occupants.

It should also not be located in the northwest because, in feng shui calculations, this sector represents the metal element and the head of the household. The fire generated will melt the metal and cause health problems and work obstacles for the man of the house. Having a kitchen in the south will increase the likelihood of fire outbreaks or related accidents.

The kitchen should not be visible from the main entrance. Some feng shui masters feel this may result in a leakage of wealth, which the stove generates, while others believe that if the occupants see the kitchen on entering their home, their appetite will be stimulated, causing them to overeat and become obese.

Traditional feng shui masters are cautious about open-plan kitchens because they feel the wealth generated by the stove may easily dissipate. In addition, stoves in the centre of the kitchen (in an island, for example) are considered negative as they lack backing and, therefore, support.

Column No 88: November 19, 2006

Attics and Basements (Up and Under)

To increase our living space, attics and basements are often used inappropriately in our homes. Basements are excessively yin areas, especially when the windows are narrow, small, or non-existent, preventing natural sunlight (yang energy) from streaming in. They are also susceptible to dampness as the ventilation may be poor. It is not advisable to use basements as bedrooms because occupants will have an increased incidence of yin-related illnesses such as arthritis and impaired memory.

Using a basement as a study is also not advisable, as the yin energy present will affect one's focus and concentration. Ideally, the basement area can be used as a storage space or a play area for extremely active children who will benefit from the calming yin energy. Note that a basement should be well lit and ventilated to increase its yang energy.

You should use attics and loft spaces as a bedroom only if there is significant light filtering through the windows and the floor-to-ceiling height is at least two and a half metres. You should ensure that the bed is not placed along or underneath any structural beams.

While attics may be used as storage spaces, you should not store anything very heavy there, especially not above a bed or desk on the level below.

Column No 122: July 29, 2007

Guest Rooms (The Perfect Host)

While many of us are able to offer visitors only the couch to stay on for a few nights, some people have sufficient space for a guest room.

Classical feng shui masters recommend a guest room not be located in the sector of your home with the most beneficial energy, the reason being that this positive energy will not be stimulated adequately. It is also unfair to put a guest room in the area with negative energy (the sickness sector) as guests may develop ailments or other problems.

It is acceptable to combine another function with the guest room, such as a television room or study. This will ensure the room is frequently utilised, allowing for adequate circulation of chi and optimal use of space. It is not advisable for children to move into their parents' room when there are visitors, as this will deprive the children of their own space, causing them to feel unsettled.

To prevent stagnant yin energy from accumulating in a guest room, clean it regularly and don't use it to store junk. If the guest room is in the most auspicious sector of your home, your guests may become so comfortable they won't want to leave.

Column No 153: March 16, 2008

Toilets and Wealth (Myth Busting)

Just as there are urban legends, there are also feng shui fallacies that have become ingrained in our psyche. You may have heard, for instance, that the toilet lid should be kept down at all times to prevent your wealth from being flushed away, and that this particularly applies if your toilet is located in the southeast, the wealth sector of your home. In reality, these ideas have no basis in traditional feng shui.

The wealth sector is not always located in the southeast of the home. Rather, its location is obtained from calculations involving the orientation (sitting and facing directions) of the property and the time at which it was completed. Some feng shui masters will also determine the wealth sector as per the occupants' year of birth.

If the wealth sector of your home is where the toilet is located, don't worry; this sector is stimulated through activity and light.

Using a dehumidifier or a fan in your bathroom will activate the auspicious energy present. When the bathroom is unoccupied, keep the door ajar unless it points towards you when you are in bed. If this is the case, keep the toilet door closed at night.

Natural light can also stimulate the beneficial energy but don't believe what you hear about aquariums and water fountains having the same effect.

Column No 157: April 13, 2008

Extensions and Additions (Home Improvements)

Walling in a balcony and incorporating the area into your living space will have an effect on the overall feng shui of your home. Whether this will be positive or negative depends on the location of the balcony. For instance, if the wealth sector is where the balcony was, incorporating it into your living space will be a positive move.

In feng shui, balconies are considered external – areas where occupants spend very little time. So, the effect of an open balcony is negligible.

If you live in a flat, the new addition will probably not add more than 20 per cent to your overall living space, which means it will not need to have a separate time chart based on its construction.

However, if you live in a house, a new structural addition to the property – especially one that is free standing – will have to have its own chart.

If the new addition is incorporated into the house but shares the same entrance and exit, the original chart still applies.

These home improvements are effective in addressing any missing sectors of your property. For those living in apartments, renovations need to take into account the approval of your building committee and neighbours – and it's worth bearing in mind that any work that disrupts the external appearance of your building will change the overall feng shui.

Column No 182: October 5, 2008

Kitchen Appliances (The Science of Appliance)

There is a school of thinking in feng shui that states the electricity that enters your kitchen appliances should be oriented from one of the directions that suits you.

For instance, if east is a beneficial direction for you, the cords for your kettle, rice cooker or microwave should enter the appliance from the east. This type of practice has no basis in traditional feng shui, and it really doesn't matter which direction electricity enters an appliance.

Another common fallacy is that the dials on the stove should be positioned specifically according to a person's 'good' direction, based on their year of birth. For instance, believers might insist oven switches lie against a northern wall. This has resulted in unusual and impractical requests for dials and controls to stove manufacturers, but the positioning of electrical or gas stove switches is of no consequence.

Then there is the belief that your stove should back into one of the favourable directions of the head of the household. However, placing the stove at an awkward angle to fulfill this criterion will just result in disputes between family members.

Column No 211: May 10, 2009

Modern Kitchens (Cooking By the Book)

When feng shui principles relating to the kitchen were conceived, they obviously could not take into account modern innovations.

The traditional stove had to be kept clean and operational at all times, as it was believed to be where one's wealth was generated. To prevent that wealth from escaping, a solid wall behind the stove in a modern kitchen is preferable. If your stove has a mirror or shiny reflective tiles behind it, then a degree of instability is introduced, which may translate to financial and health problems.

Similar problems will occur if your stove has a window behind it that allows you to enjoy spectacular views when cooking; in these circumstances, consider reorienting the stove or blocking part of the view to simulate a solid wall when you are cooking.

Island stoves - those located in the centre of the kitchen - lack backing. Consider placing something solid – such as a rack or a stack of cooking books – behind such a structure to provide some support for the stove.

Open-plan kitchens are not considered ideal in traditional feng shui as they do not allow energy to accumulate in the preparation area.

Remember, a clear view of the outside world normally means trouble.

Column No 212: May 17, 2009

Balconies (Outer Space)

Balconies are an integral part of many modern apartments. However, when it comes to feng shui, they are not considered part of a home, as they are open to the elements. Chi is unable to accumulate on a balcony and will scatter; enclosing it may allow beneficial energy, such as wealth or romance *chi*, to be incorporated into a home, but this depends on the orientation and layout of the apartment.

Do not use your balcony as a storeroom; *chi* from your home may not be able to exit or circulate due to the physical blockage, leading to a sense of stagnation within the home.

You may raise the yang energy of a balcony by placing potted plants there but ensure they grow well and are not left to wither and die.

If the wealth sector of your apartment happens to be where the balcony is, putting a water feature on it will not be effective. Instead, place the feature just inside the balcony doors, within your living space.

Column No 221: July 19, 2009

Octagons (Rules of the Table)

You may have seen the octagon (eight sided) design on the feng shui or *Pa Kua* mirrors, adorned with Chinese characters, that are hung outside the entrance to homes or offices. They confer protection against negative forces or energy. The octagon encompasses the four cardinal (north, south, east and west) and four inter-cardinal (northeast, northwest, southeast and southwest) directions.

In traditional feng shui formulas, family members are each assigned a specific direction, i.e. the father is associated with the northwest, the mother the southwest, the oldest son the east, the middle daughter the south and so on.

It is incorrect to assume that you should have an octagonal dining table in your home. Rectangular, square, oval or round tables are all appropriate for the dining room, while triangular or irregular tables are not recommended.

It is also wrong to assume that the father, or head of the household, should always sit in the northwest part of the table and the mother the southwest; it is unreasonable to allocate each family member to a certain place at the dining table based only on their rank in the family. Other factors, such as the position of the table relative to walls, doors and passageways, should be taken into account to determine who should sit where.

Column No 222: July 26, 2009

Shoes (Life and Sole)

Often in Hong Kong and Singapore, shoes are kept either in cabinets right outside a home or next to the front door. Rather than wearing shoes in the home, slippers or even bare feet are preferred.

While there is obviously a hygiene element to the decision to keep shoes out of a living space, it is also believed that shoes pick up energy or *chi* from places you visit. If you have visited places with intense spiritual or emotional energy, such as hospitals, temples or law courts, then negative energy associated with sorrow, disputes and worry may linger on your footwear. Leaving your shoes at the front door as you enter will ensure that any external *chi* that you may have come across your travels will be limited to an outside area of your home.

There are feng shui masters who stipulate that shoe cabinets should not be above waist level. This is not necessarily true for modern living. What is more important is that the shoe cabinet is proportional to the size of the room it stands in, and the home itself. Having a shoe cabinet that covers the entire height and breadth of your entrance hall is not recommended as it will overwhelm the entrance.

Column No 230: September 20, 2009

Chapter 15

Spiritual Matters

Altars/Symbols of Significance (Object Lessons)

Regardless of one's personal beliefs, feng shui guidelines should be followed when it comes to the placement of religious objects in the home. These principles also apply to where you place objects of personal significance, such as family photos, carvings or statues of deities. Placing these objects directly opposite the front door is good as they can protect the home. It is disrespectful to place them on the floor or below waist height.

Statues or photos should not be placed with their backs to the front door or passageways where there is much movement and activity. Placing them opposite the toilet or kitchen door is also not recommended. It's best to place them in a semi-public space such as a hall or living room rather than your bedroom. Religious statues should not be placed with their backs to a wall with a toilet or stove behind, or below staircases where people can walk over their heads.

The same principles extend to altars; they should not be located at the end of long passageways or be placed under overhanging beams. Keep electrical equipment such as televisions and stereo systems separate from altars. Be mindful of the beliefs of others; it would be unwise to place a statue of Buddha in your toilet.

Column No 15: June 12, 2005

Cemeteries and Temples (Dead Calm)

Having your house next to a cemetery or graveyard is not advisable for several reasons. It's best to keep the yang and yin worlds, in other words, those of the living and the dead, separate. The mixing of yin and yang causes complications resulting from excessive yin energy, such as poor health, lethargy and fatigue. In such circumstances, there will also be an increased number of supernatural occurrences, which should not be taken lightly.

In certain parts of Hong Kong, there are clusters of residential buildings in the vicinity of cemeteries, with occupants who not only enjoy good health, but also career success. This could well be explained by the fact these graveyards have not been used for a number of years and the reduced yin energy calms residents instead.

Churches and temples are also areas of yin activity. Places of worship tend to draw in the yang energy from their immediate environs. These are also places where visitors come to terms with their spiritual and existential anxieties, thereby creating a focus of unsettled energy that will affect neighbouring residents. Thus, it is best to avoid living in the vicinity of excessively yin areas such as churches, temples and cemeteries that are still in use.

Column No 38: November 20, 2005

Fuk Luk Sau (Favourable Figurines)

While browsing in Hong Kong's shops, you may have come across the figurines of the Chinese equivalent of the three wise men: Fuk, Luk and Sau. They can be bought in a wide variety of sizes and materials, including jade, porcelain and silver. While you may be aware they represent fortune, prosperity and longevity, respectively, chances are you are not be familiar with how and where they should be placed.

Fuk should always be located in the centre of the three. Dressed in a green and red robe, he is easily identified by his slightly protruding abdomen, which suggests the enjoyment of a fortunate life. Luk wears a blue robe and will be holding either a scroll or a child. The former is a symbol of academic and professional success, while the latter signifies healthy descendants and continuation of the family lineage.

When facing the figurines, Luk should be on the left. Finally, Sau is usually clothed in yellow and will be holding either one or both of the symbols of longevity: a cane and a peach. Ideally, Fuk, Luk and Sau should be placed off the floor and in a public area such as the living or dining room.

Should any of the figures be broken, it is believed that particular aspect of life will be adversely affected. If this happens, purchase a new set of figurines.

Column No 42: December 18, 2005

Haunted Houses

When moving house, it is important to know the history of the property and that of its previous occupants, especially if unfortunate events such as bankruptcy, divorce, illness or even murder have occurred there. In terms of feng shui, there are certain risk factors in a property that could predispose it to the occurrence of specific events, regardless of the year of birth of the occupants.

Risk factors could be structural: if the front door of an apartment leads directly onto a balcony, new occupants may face the financial ruin that probably befell the previous occupants. At times, risk factors may not be immediately evident: for instance, there could be a toilet located in the wealth sector.

If a tragic incident, such as suicide or murder, occurred on the premises, it would not be advisable to move in without major modifications being made because feng shui calculations, based on the age of a home and its orientation, will probably indicate it is prone to these particular unfortunate events.

In such circumstances, a major renovation is advisable because it would change the 'age' of the property. The negative energy left over from a tragic event would also need to be cleared. This can be done with the help of experts trained in the spiritual realm, which is beyond the scope of a traditional feng shui master.

Column No 44: January 8, 2006

Talismans (Bless this House)

If you live in Asia, the chances are you have across Taoist talismans: pieces of paper bearing written or painted inscriptions or symbols that can repel negative spiritual forces. They are used to purify an environment or structure. Some large talismans are prominently displayed in the lobbies of hotels and office buildings while others are pocket sized.

Drawn with a peach-wood pen by Taoist priests, or those trained in the spiritual arts, talismans usually contain Chinese characters in the traditional script, in knots and strings that might represent star constellations. They also feature seals and illustrations of the heads of gods, emperors and animals. You can obtain them from temples, religious shops or from the pages of Chinese almanacs.

Traditionally, talismans are written then blessed by priests, who give them to clients. Buildings situated on grounds that were previously associated with suffering and death, such as cemeteries, funeral parlours, slaughterhouses, morgues and hospitals, or where occupants may have suffered untimely or accidental deaths, will benefit from the placement of such blessed talismans. The building's karma will also need to be cleansed through specific prayers and rituals.

Column No 115: June 10, 2007

Buddha Statues (With all Due Respect)

You may have some Buddha figurines in your home that you bought while traveling. Buddha, a Sanskrit word, means "a person who has reached enlightenment." As we all have the potential for enlightenment, Buddhas are not considered deities, but teachers.

You may have noticed differences in Buddha statues from country to country. Thai Buddhas are usually slim and seated in contemplation while Chinese Buddhas are plump and may carry a sack of gold.

Regardless of the type you have, feng shui principles apply to their placement. They should only be put in certain rooms: the entrance hall, study, living and dining rooms. The bedroom is for sleeping and intimacy – putting Buddha figures here is inappropriate, as is placing them in the bathroom or toilet.

They should be above waist height. Placing them on the floor is inadvisable – feet may brush against them, denoting a lack of respect. There are no specific directions in which the Buddhas should face, as long as they are not opposite internal doors or at the end of a long corridor.

Column No 169: July 6, 2008

Marriage Rites (Conjugal Rites)

Before the end of the Qing dynasty in 1911, the six marriage rites were strictly adhered to in China. Tradition dictated the man's family would make the initial approach to the woman - never the other way around. A go-between, who could be a family member, friend or professional, will then take a token present to the would-be bride's family with the man's birth details on a piece of red paper. This was the first rite, *na cai*: when the present was accepted it indicated the proposal was being considered. The second rite, *wen ming*, occurred when the woman's family gave her birth data to the go-between to be presented to the man's family.

The third rite, *na ji*, which means 'acceptance of the propitious', occurred after the astrological data of the future bride and groom had been analyzed and considered compatible by a professional. This constituted a betrothal that should not be broken except by mutual agreement. The fourth rite, *na zheng*, or 'acceptance of evidence', was when there was an exchange of presents between both parties. The fifth rite, *qing qi*, 'asking the date', was usually carried out by the man's family, who consulted a professional for an auspicious time and date for the wedding. When the date and time were accepted by the woman's family, the sixth and final rite, *ying qing*, or 'receiving the bride', took place.

Column No 235: October 25, 2009

Marriage Customs (Paying Respects)

Marriage customs such as those involving the bridal chair and carriages are no longer relevant but receiving of the groom and the tea ceremony are still widely practiced in Hong Kong.

The groom and his groomsmen call at the home or hotel room where the bride is waiting with her bridesmaids or young relatives such as nephews or nieces. The bridesmaids may obstruct the groom's party from entering the room until they are paid off with *lai see* packets. The groom finally enters the room to be received by his bride.

The bride is then taken to her new home by the groom where they pay respects to his ancestors and elders. The couple must bow before the household gods and ancestral tablets. They are also instructed to bow in each of the four cardinal directions to honour heaven and earth. Following this, they pay respects to family members during a tea ceremony.

Older relatives sit opposite the bride and groom, who will bow or kneel as they offer their elders a cup of tea. The elders reciprocate by accepting and then drinking the tea before giving the couple a red packet, which may contain jewellery instead of money. The tea ceremony is applicable to both the bride's and groom's relatives, welcoming each to their new family.

Column No 236: November 1, 2009

Mourning Rites (Rites of Passage)

Traditionally, upon the death of a family member, a feng shui master will be consulted with regard to the most auspicious hour and day for the funeral and cremation and for the burial or internment of ashes.

Close family members are present when the body is placed in the coffin, which will be lined with paper, clothes or other materials, depending upon the wishes of the deceased. The lid is then nailed and sealed by a professional undertaker, who will utter blessings while doing so.

The coffin will be kept in the house or funeral parlour for a few days to enable friends and relatives to pay their last respects. An altar for praying is set up in front of the coffin and decorated with wreaths of white or blue (never red) flowers. Buddhist or Taoist monks are employed to chant prayers at appointed hours. Food is offered at the altar at meal times in accordance with filial piety rituals: the Chinese serve dead elders the same way they do the living.

When visitors come to pay their respects, the deceased's descendants kneel (males on one side, females on the other) to show their respect to the visitors.

A banquet may also be thrown for the mourners. Visitors bring gifts in the form of wreaths, cash in white envelopes, and banners or scrolls with words of praise for the deceased that bear the details of the giver.

Column No 237: November 8, 2009

Funeral Rites (Ashes to Ashes)

On the day of a funeral, as specified by a feng shui master, relatives and friends gather in front of an altar set up in front of the coffin to pay their last respects. Food offerings are made and paper money burnt so that the deceased will have some cash in the next world.

Paper imitations of possessions such as watches and houses can also be burnt and offered to the deceased. The timing of the funeral procession is vital, as the coffin needs to arrive at the cemetery for burial at a specified auspicious hour.

The funeral procession is led by a pair of large white lanterns on poles that bear the surname and age of the deceased. Behind the lanterns should be a portable altar containing the ancestral tablet and a photograph of the deceased, carried by the children or grandchildren. The main funeral procession may have had a brass band or musical troupe preceding the coffin and the family.

At the cemetery, incense, joss paper and food offerings are made to the god in charge of the deceased. Following this ceremony, the coffin is lowered into the grave and family members throw lumps of earth on top of it.

The ancestral tablet is taken home and the family returns three days later to ensure the interment has taken place without incident.

Column No 238: November 15, 2009

Ancestral Tablets (In Memoriam)

You may have noticed ancestral tablets that can be found in homes across Asia. They consist of an upright piece of flat wood standing on a wooden pedestal. Both the pedestal and the borders of the table bear elaborate designs. On the centre of the tablet is written the name of the ancestor (containing the generation name that is used to identify their seniority within the family or clan) and the year in which he/she was born. Older tablets may mention the year of the reigning emperor of a specific dynasty. The characters for 'spiritual seat', *shen wei*, may be present and the date of the ancestor's death is also recorded.

The Chinese believe that a person has three souls: one remains in the earth after burial, one will be reincarnated and the third resides in the ancestral tablet. The tablet is kept and worshipped by the family for three to five generations but never beyond five. Some families prefer to place the tablet at a clan hall or temple and pay respects to their ancestors at these venues on important days of the year, such as the Ching Ming festival.

The tablet may have elaborate animal and floral designs and some are even gilded.

The names of the descendants who erected the tablet are written at the bottom, to the left of the ancestor's name.

Column No 239: November 22, 2009

Confucianism (Being Human)

Feng Shui is but one of a number of codes that Chinese have traditionally lived by. Confucianism is another. It is a philosophy concerning human relationships and conduct, but is not a religion. It is best described as humanism and is primarily concerned with social interaction rather than the divine or spiritual afterlife.

Confucius was born in 551 BC during the Warring States period in what is now Shandong Province. He became renowned for his theories and teachings on human behaviour, conduct and forms of government. He emphasized *li*, which means 'ritual' or 'propriety'. This included filial piety, respect for ancestors and the observance of rites. Hence, ancestral worship is not related to the spiritual world but rather an act of filial piety, stressing the importance of the perpetuation of the family unit from which a nation draws its strength.

This philosophy is reflected in the term for nation, *guo jia*, which means 'country and family'. Thus, the junior member of a family or work team must respect the senior and the senior must be kind to the junior. A good government has to be run by those who set an example for others to follow, resulting in progress.

The other important Confucian concepts are *yi* (morality or duty) and *ren*, which means benevolence and kindness towards your fellow man. After all, as Confucius said, what can one do with propriety (*li*) without any (*ren*) universal love?

Confucianism's humanistic philosophies don't share any theories with feng shui, unlike Taoism which does.

Column No 240: November 29, 2009

Taoism (Go with the Flow)

The word *Tao* means 'way', which may refer to a path, a way of life, or a discipline that is followed closely. It is also a power that transcends any reality conceived by the human mind and is the central force to which all objects and forces return in their cycles of death and rebirth. Natural revolves in a perpetual cycle that spins outward from the tao to all creatures and then back to the tao for renewal, in keeping with the turn of the seasons.

Yin and yang are the basic aspects of the tao, as are the *wu xing*: the five elements that occur naturally. Yin (gentleness) and yang (strength) are the complementary opposites of the same reality and overlap and mix to produce balance. Water, wood, fire, metal and earth shape the world and are used to classify all types of relationships, such as those involving directions, seasons, tastes, body organs, colours etc.

Another central concept of Taoism is chi, the energy that gives life to all cosmic beings and creatures. It is a manifestation of the power of the tao and streams throughout the cosmic environment and the individual.

Chinese medicine addresses the flow of chi within the body while feng shui deals with the flow of chi within your immediate environment. Thus, feng shui theories are derived from Taoist concepts, but one does not need to be a Taoist in order to benefit from them.

Column No 241: December 6, 2009

Buddhism (Finding Nirvana)

Buddhism originated in India in about 500BC and spread along the Silk Road to China through missionaries in the first century AD, gaining popularity after the fall of the Han Dynasty, in 220 AD. Buddha - the Enlightened or Awakened One - was born into the wealthy Gautama family and named Siddharta. The traditional story is that he abandoned his comfortable life at the age of 29 in favour of a more spiritual path and achieved enlightenment while mediating under a Bo tree.

The central tenet of Buddhism - the Four Noble Truths - holds that existence consists of suffering; that suffering is caused by attachment or desire; that there is a way to end this suffering; and that is to follow the Eightfold Path. This means having the right view, intention, speech, action, livelihood, effort, mindfulness and concentration. The concept of karma or action, was linked to the five groups or *skandhas* that make up a person: body, feelings, consciousness, perceptions and impulses. These five will be reconfigured in a better or worse way in the future depending on the good or bad acts that one performs in the present. The aim is to exit from the cosmic cycle of reincarnation through the attainment of Nirvana, when desire, hate and delusion have all been extinguished.

Buddhism gained popularity in China as it addressed questions about death and spirituality that were not answered by Confucianism and Taoism. However, feng shui's philosophies are derived from Taoism rather than either Confucianism or Buddhism.

Column No 242: December 13, 2009

Co-existence of Philosophies (Three in One)

The Chinese approach to religion is best summed up in the saying, "three religions, one religion", whereby Confucianism, Taoism and Buddhism co-exist. For example, a person may follow Confucius in his interactions with his family and colleagues by maintaining relationships based on mutual respect and love; the teachings of Taoism and Lao Tzu by not striving for things he cannot get, thereby respecting the yin/yang balance of the universe and strengthening and cultivating his own character; and Buddhism when he performs good deeds with benevolent intentions, auguring well for his life after death.

The intertwining of these three philosophies can also be seen in feng shui. While feng shui shares Taoist principles and cosmology (i.e. chi, yin/yang, the five elements), it also takes account of the other two philosophies. For instance, neither Buddha statues nor ancestral tablets and photographs should be placed in areas where there is negative chi, such as at the end of corridors or in toilets and washrooms. Objects with religious and personal significance should be kept above floor level, where feet or shoes may come into contact with them, and above the level of the waist, to show respect. They should not be placed in bedrooms, as this is an area for personal intimacy.

Another example of the coming of together of the belief systems can be found at funerals held at an auspicious time and day (as determined by feng shui) with Buddhist and Taoist monks present to chant prayers for the deceased.

Column No 243: December 20, 2009

Chapter 16

Chinese Astrology

The Sexagenary Cycle (Think Pig)

It was widely reported in the media that 2006 was the Year of the Golden or Metal Pig and that 2010 was the year of the Tiger. However, those in the feng shui industry know that was actually the Year of the Fire Pig. So how many kinds of pigs are there?

In Chinese astrology, each of the 12 animals of the zodiac can be assigned to any of the five elements. Thus, there are five types of pigs: the wood, fire, earth, metal and water pig. With this classification, there are 60 types of animals, also known as the sexagenary cycle. The cycle starts with the wood rat, runs through the next 58 animals then ends with the water pig, before starting again with the wood rat.

Hence, it was considered an important event in ancient China when one lived to the age of 60 as he or she had gone through all the different animals and types of energy and had therefore lived a full life. Each additional year after the age of 60 was considered a bonus.

Feng Shui masters are also able to correlate the final digit of the year of birth with one's element. For instance, wood years end with the digits '4' or '5'. Those still alive today and born in the wood pig year would thus have been born in 1995 or 1935. This information is also used to predict a person's character in Chinese astrology.

Column No 123: August 5, 2007

New Year Predictions (Smell a Rat)

With the approach of the Chinese New, numerous articles predicting one's fortune in the New Year appear, and are readily available, in print and online. Due to space constraints, these articles just provide an overview of the year by assigning everyone to one of 12 Chinese zodiac animals.

While there are undeniably truths in these predictions, the casual reader should be aware that they are not entirely accurate as they do not take into account the full astrological data of one's birth. The *paht chee* or Eight Characters assigns a specific element and a zodiac animal for one's birth hour, day, month and year to provide a complete picture. Also known as the Four Pillars of Destiny, these charts are used by astrologers not only to predict one's fortune through the years, but also to assess compatibility between individuals in marriage and business partnerships. In this system, the main governing factor is not the year of birth, but the day.

Hence, it is incorrect to assume that all those born in the Year of the Horse will have a bad year in 2008. Similarly, it is unwise to declare that everyone with the rat as their zodiac sign will have a great year. Indeed, to have a reliable picture of your fortune for the New Year, it's best to consult an experienced astrologer.

Column No 146: January 20, 2008

Chinese Astrology (Off the Chart)

Feng shui accounts for the effect of the environment, or the 'earth luck' component of one's life. To measure the 'heaven luck' or preordained aspects of our lives, the Chinese use astrology. The best-known method is the *Shang Chung Paht Chee*, or the Eight Characters, or the Four Pillars of Destiny. The astrological chart of one's birth is derived from the Ten Thousand-year Calendar, which shows the element-animal combination for the year, month, day and hour of birth. The element refers to either the yin or yang component of one of the five elements, while the animal is one of the 12 animals of the Chinese zodiac.

When the four elements and four animals are lined up side by side on the chart, the practitioner is able to more reliably assess a person's character and personality. The governing pillar is that of the day of birth, as opposed to the year. This accounts for the differences in fortune that those born in the same year may experience in a specific year.

Charts are also used to assess compatibility between individuals, professionally and personally. For instance, a common practice in ancient China, that is still prevalent today, is for families to analyse the birth charts of prospective spouses for their children, to determine their marriage prospects.

Column No 166: June 15, 2008

Astrology Charts (Life in Balance)

From a person's *paht chee*, or Eight Characters astrological chart, the feng shui master decides which elements are useful and which are undesirable, and gives advice accordingly on such areas such as career and health.

For instance, a person who requires fire to give balance in their chart should choose fire-related professions such as cooking, chemical engineering, advertising and photography. Those who have earth as the undesirable element are advised not to work in the property sector, or speculate in real estate.

With regard to health, the principles of Chinese medicine are applied to the chart. For instance, those who have excessive water in their charts may suffer from bladder, kidney and blood problems, while those with a compromised metal element will be prone to ailments of the lungs and brain.

Auspicious elements are used to determine the most appropriate colours for the individual. Those who benefit from the earth element are advised to wear earth tones such as brown and beige while those who find the fire element overwhelming should refrain from driving red cars, as this may increase their likelihood of accidents.

Some masters use the charts to determine the best directions in which to face while sleeping and working. For example, if a person requires wood to restore equilibrium, they should sleep with their head in the direction associated with that element, such as southeast.

Column No 167: June 22, 2008

Astrology Clashes (Character Clash)

You may have read or heard that a person born in the Year of the Rat should never marry someone born in the Year of the Horse, as the clash between these two animals will eventually lead to divorce. The rat-horse clash is one of six within the Chinese zodiac, the other five pairs being the ox-sheep, tiger-monkey, rabbit-rooster, dragon-dog and snake-pig. This phenomenon is also employed in feng shui to determine unsuitable and suitable directions for individuals.

However, in astrology, writing off a relationship based simply on the years of birth does not take into account the overall picture. When Chinese astrologers analyse the characters of their clients and a prospective spouse or business partner, they also take into account the month, day and hour of birth. Instead of focusing on any particular animals, the consultant considers the five elements (wood, fire, earth, metal and water) present within the charts. For instance, the presence of fire may be extremely strong in a person's chart, and he or she will therefore need water to restore equilibrium. Partnering with another person who has considerable fire within their chart would not be a good thing to do, because conflicts may arise in the future.

Astrology is just part of the picture and provides a guide towards the compatibility of individuals. Even if the elements within two charts are favourable, a lot of effort and understanding is required to make any long-term relationship work.

Column No 168: June 29, 2008

Chinese Ages (Age Factor)

When it comes to one's age, in Chinese astrology - and even in general conversation with a Chinese individual - it is usually given as at least a year more than in western tradition. For instance, a child born in November will, in Chinese terms, turn two at the start of the following Lunar New Year. By western calculations he or she would only be 1½ months.

Note that others take into account the winter solstice as the start of a New Year, which means, by this calculation, that everyone becomes a year older on December 21.

This discrepancy can be attributed to the belief that when a child is born, he is already nine or so months old, because age is counted from conception. There are actually Chinese terms that take into account this difference: one's age in western terms is known as the *shi* or 'real' age, while the Chinese age is known as the *xu* or 'empty' age.

Bear in mind that you'll have to add a year to your age when consulting Chinese astrologers or reading astrology manuals.

Column No 187: November 9, 2008

The Ten Thousand Year Calendar (Long-term View)

You may have seen the *Wan Nian Li* (*Man Nien Lik* in Cantonese) or *Ten Thousand Year Calendar* on sale in bookshops but be unclear as to what its purpose is. It is usually printed like a compact dictionary, and is used by feng shui masters to compile the astrological data of individuals, allowing them to calculate, among other things, the compatibility of two people with regard to a business partnership or marriage, or the suitability of a home or office for a person.

The calendar shouldn't be confused with the *Tong Seng*, which is the annual Chinese almanac which identifies favourable and unfavourable activities for each day of a specific year.

In contrast, the *Ten Thousand Year Calendar*, despite its name, usually covers a period of more than a hundred years, for example from 1912 until 2050, identifying the stem and branch or element and animal combination for each and every day, month and year.

As data for future dates is also provided, feng shui masters are able to advise parents as to the most appropriate time for their children to be born if they choose a Caesarean birth, for example, by consulting the book.

The calendar also serves as a reference for occasions that reoccur annually, such as Lunar New Year, Tomb Sweeping Day and the Mid-Autumn Festival and Dragon Boat festivals.

Column No 231: September 27, 2009

Luck Cycles in Astrology (A Matter of Luck)

You may heard it said that someone is going through a good-luck or bad-luck cycle but not understand what it means. Chinese astrologers are able to forecast the ups and downs of a person's life, right down to specifics that might occur in a particular year. Under the *paht chee* (or Eight Characters) system of astrology, luck cycles last for five years and are represented by one of the five elements (wood, metal, fire, earth and water) or one of the 12 Chinese zodiac animals. Each of the animals represents one, two or three elements. For instance, the rat contains only the water element, while the ox represents metal, earth and water.

So how is this information used by the astrologer? The overall pattern of a birth chart is first determined by looking at the four elements and the four animals (the eight characters) that constitute a chart, which is derived from the time, day, month and year of a person's birth.

More calculations will then yield the ages at which one's luck cycles will change and the elements or animals that will govern the new cycle. An experienced feng shui master will be able to identify the positive and negative elements for the person and thus determine whether he or she will enjoy good fortune or face adversity during each five year-period.

Column No 246: January 17, 2010

Traveling Tiger (Going Places)

The Year of the Tiger is a year that will signify movement for those who were born in the years of the monkey, rat and dragon, as the tiger is the animal that represents movement or travel.

Those of us that were born in those years can expect to rove more than usual in 2010 or perhaps move to a new home or country. Note that 2010 here refers to the Chinese solar year, which runs from February 4, 2010 to February 3, 2011.

The other three animals in the Chinese zodiac that signify travel are the snake, monkey and pig. For those born in a year of the tiger, horse or dog, the year associated with travel would be that of the monkey.

In a year of the pig, those born in a year of the snake, rooster or ox will be affected.

In the next year of the snake (2013), it will be the turn of those born in the pig, rabbit or sheep years to step up their traveling.

Column No 247: January 24, 2010

Astrological Romance (Lucky in Love)

We have looked at ways of encouraging romance through the placement of water features or plants – but there is another way. The romance sector for an individual is determined by referring to the Chinese zodiac animal of their year of birth.

For those born in the years of the monkey, rat or dragon, the romance sector lies in the west. It lies in the east for those belonging to the years of the tiger, horse and dog. If you happen to be a snake, rooster or ox, then your 'peach blossom' sector is located in the south, while those born in the years of the pig, rabbit or sheep must look to the north.

Once you have identified your romance sector, look at the corresponding sector in your home. What is there? Monkeys looking for love, for instance, are advised to place images or symbols associated with romance – prints of happy couples, flowers and even fish – in the western sector of their home. An experienced feng shui master will be able to recommend the number, type and colour of flower or fish you should use.

For a more accurate indication of when you are likely to be lucky in love, your date of birth as per the Chinese *Ten-Thousand Year Calendar* should be analysed and compared with the element energy and zodiac animal of the year.

Column No 249: February 7, 2010

275

Tiger Women (Cat Women)

Some men are reluctant to marry women born in a Year of the Tiger as they believe them to be fierce and domineering. This belief is clearly not true, otherwise all women born in 1938, 1950, 1962, 1974, 1986, 1998 and 2010 would, or will, make poor wives. If such a statement were true, then those women born in the snake years would be venomous and those born in a Year of the Pig would be slobs. It would be wrong to call off an engagement based on such fallacies.

These ideas became prevalent due to a misguided tendency to apply characteristics associated with the Chinese zodiac animals to individuals born in their years. To ascertain the suitability of a potential life partner, their entire astrological chart should be considered – including the time, day, month and year of birth – either through the *paht chee* (Eight Characters) system or the *zi wei dou shu* (Emperor or purple star astrology) method.

The *paht chee* method provides an indication of one's relationship to one's spouse and the compatibility of two individuals based on their mutual positive or negative elements. The latter system is an indicator of marriage luck and personal thinking with regard to relationships.

If you are, indeed, married to an aggressive, dominating woman born in a year of the striped cat, you are merely unlucky – you have not been bitten by the tiger.

Column No 250: February 21, 2010

Baby Animals (Birth Control)

Some people have a preference for babies born under a certain sign; the rat and dragon are extremely popular because the former is the first animal of the zodiac cycle and the latter is considered the most powerful and auspicious of all the creatures.

In 2007 there was a misinformed rush in Hong Kong to have 'golden pig babies'; but it was actually the Year of the Fire (rather than metal/golden) Pig, because a certain journalist had not done his homework properly, and many people took him at his word.

The Year of the Tiger is not considered to be a popular one, as it is believed by some people that children born under this sign will be aggressive and bad tempered. That is an irrational fear because deciding whether a child will bring fortune or adversity to its parents is properly done by referring to the time, day and month of birth, not just the year. Babies are not like fashion trends; they aren't hot or not depending on the season.

Experienced astrologers can analyse astrology charts to identify the years when a woman's chances of falling pregnant will be highest – and that may well not be in a Year of the Rat or Dragon. By waiting for a preferred animal year, a woman may reduce her chance of falling pregnant at all. Babies should be valued and appreciated as blessings, regardless of which Chinese zodiac sign they belong to.

Column No 253: March 14, 2010

Chapter 17

Chinese Names

Chinese Surnames

The Chinese believe a person's name can determine their destiny; that an auspicious name will bring forth prosperity and achievement while an inappropriate one may prevent the individual from enjoying a good life.

Chinese names usually consist of three characters, the family name or surname preceding the generation name and the final character indicating the personal name. The importance of roots, clans or family is evident in the fact the surname comes first. The emphasis is therefore on the group as opposed to the individual.

Surnames may be derived from a region or village in China in which one's ancestors originated. The *Bai Jia Xin*, or *Book of A Hundred Names*, lists the county and province of origin of 100 surnames. However, some Chinese names are not listed in this compendium.

Some surnames consist of two characters, such as Ow Yang, Shang Guan and Si Ma. In such instances, the person may have three or four characters in total in their name or both the generation and personal names. Note that those with a single character surname may also forgo the generation name, resulting in a two-character name.

Column No 176: August 24, 2008

Naming Rules (What's in a Name?)

There are general rules to consider with regard to Chinese names. First and foremost, they have to be easy to pronounce. If all three characters have the same consonant or vowel, the name will be difficult to enunciate. Characters with different consonants that may be similar in sound should also be avoided. Nor should characters be of the same tone, otherwise the name may sound ungainly.

With regard to the characters when written, those that are extremely complex with too many strokes should be avoided; otherwise children and others will find them difficult to write. Besides which, the name may be difficult to decipher. Names that have too few strokes are also to be avoided, as they appear weak, coarse and lacking in form when written.

Constructing a name from characters that are rarely used is not recommended, as this will cause others to mispronounce or forget it. The ideal Chinese names are those that are balanced in terms of number of strokes and forms in tandem with the surname.

The meaning of the name is also vital. As extremely different Chinese characters may share the same pronunciation, make sure the name does not bring to mind homonyms with negative associations and connotations. At times, the overall meaning of the generation and personal names may be changed when the surname is factored in.

Column No 177: August 31, 2008

Males and Females (Gender Agenda)

Chinese names usually reflect expectations parents may have for their children: virtues such as benevolence, intelligence and perseverance. Those who have had turbulent lives may choose names that ensure a smoother existence for their children. Some parents may name their children after specific events they feel honoured to have witnessed in their lifetime, such as the Beijing Olympics.

Some characters are gender specific. For instance, boys tend to have names that denote strength, business acumen, ambition, willpower and responsibility. Males will also have a higher incidence of names associated with serving the nation or society. This simply exemplifies the role Chinese boys are expected to assume in their adult lives.

In contrast, girls are given names that are associated with tenderness, grace, chastity, virtue, beauty and elegance. Intelligence and wisdom in women are represented by Chinese characters that should not be applied to male names. This reflects the qualities parents hope their daughters will possess to become nurturing and supportive wives and mothers.

There is a clear distinction between masculine and feminine names. For instance, *mei* or *may* which represents 'beauty', is never used in a male name, otherwise the man may be ridiculed by his peers and elders.

Column No 178: September 7, 2008

5 Element Formulas (The Famous Five)

The theory of the five elements is used to determine the suitability of a Chinese name. Taking into account only the traditional (and not the simplified) form of the character, those that are formed using a number of strokes ending with one or two (that is, two, 11, 21 strokes) are of the wood element. Characters that have the total number of strokes ending with three or four are of the fire element, five or six, of earth, seven or eight, of metal, and nine or zero, of water.

For a name to be auspicious, the characters' elements should follow each other and not be in opposition to one another.

For instance, let's say that the surname consists of eight strokes, which means it will be of the metal element. The next two characters should be of supportive elements, also metal or the earth element, which gives birth to the metal element.

The element that is the child or product of the surname element is also acceptable; in this instance, metal produces water. Thus, with an eight stroke surname, there is the choice of using characters with five, six, seven, eight, nine or ten strokes next, to ensure a name conforms to the flow of elements.

Feng Shui professionals also analyse which elements are favourable for an individual from their birth chart and will choose the characters accordingly.

Column No 179: September 14, 2008

Strokes Method (Different Strokes)

Apart from by using the five elements theory, another way a feng shui master can ensure a favourable Chinese name is to match the number of strokes in each character (using only the classical form) to a specific chart. This is known as the Strokes Theory.

According to this method, the Heavenly Character refers to circumstances of birth and home environment. This is calculated by adding one to the number of strokes in a surname.

The Personal Character consists of the number of strokes in the surname and the second character of your name, which is usually the generation name. This gives an indication of one's overall destiny or fate.

The Earthly Character relates to relationships with those around us, i.e. children, spouse, colleagues and subordinates. It is calculated by adding the number of strokes in the second and third characters of one's name.

The Total Character is the total of the number of strokes of all three characters in a name and forecasts one's life after the age of 35.

Finally, the External Character predicts the relations one will have with other individuals. It is derived by subtracting the number of strokes in one's Personal Character from those in the Total Character, then adding one.

When naming a person, feng shui masters try to ensure the number in each of the five categories is a favourable one.

Column No 180: September 21, 2008

Index